Great Composers □ Great Artists

Great Composers □ Great Artists
PORTRAITS

STEWART BUETTNER

and

REINHARD G. PAULY

AMADEUS PRESS
Portland, Oregon

Acknowledgments

We gratefully acknowledge the help of Lewis &
Clark College and Amadeus Press who provided
financial assistance for the acquisition of illustrations for this book. Thanks also are due to the
many librarians, archivists, and museum cur-
ators, in the United States and abroad, who
answered questions and gave permission to use
material in their collections.

Copyright © 1992 by Amadeus Press
(an imprint of Timber Press, Inc.)
All rights reserved.

ISBN 0-931340-50-0 (cased)
ISBN 0-931340-57-8 (paper)
Printed in Hong Kong

AMADEUS PRESS
9999 S.W. Wilshire, Suite 124
Portland, Oregon 97225

Library of Congress Cataloging-in-Publication Data

Buettner, Stewart.
    Great composers--great artists : portraits / [compiled and
annotated by] Stewart Buettner and Reinhard G. Pauly.
        p.   cm.
    Includes bibliographical references and index.
    ISBN 0-931340-50-0
    1. Composers--Portraits.   I. Pauly, Reinhard G. II. Title.
ML87.B76 1992
    757--dc20   92-3155
                                                        CIP
                                                        MN

Contents

Preface

Our plan to assemble an annotated collection of musicians' portraits grew out of an agreeable professional association. Stewart Buettner is an art historian who is fond of and knowledgeable about music; Reinhard Pauly is a musician and scholar who for many years has had great curiosity about the visual arts. Our common interests led to our teaching jointly a series of courses dealing with interrelationships among the arts—a learning experience for both of us.

As we formulated our plans, we agreed to seek artistically significant portraits, by major artists, of great composers through the ages. We found such a selection to offer more insights than just another gallery of famous composers, though there are not many of these, old or new. (A five-volume collection, annotated and with a fine introduction, is Walter Salmen, *Musiker im Portrait*, Munich, 1982–83.)

Definitions of "artistically significant" and "great composers" had to be flexible, and our selections may not always fit both criteria. There were instances where the decision was difficult. Martin Luther, a composer though not a great composer, had a profound influence on the development of music because of his views on the place of music in the church and because of his musicianship as a singer and lute player. Since he was portrayed by Lucas Cranach, a major artist of his day, we included his portrait.

The "greatness" of a painter can also be defined in national or regional terms. Moritz von Schwind, Viktor Tilgner, Franz von Lenbach, and Max Klinger are very well known in Germany and Austria but less so in France, Italy, and the United States.

Other considerations have affected the scope of this book. There are few if any portraits of famous composers, done by famous artists, before the mid- or even late Renaissance. Earlier artists were fond of portraying musicians, but usually not identifiable ones in the sense that portraits are likenesses. Many great works of art depict men, women, and children (and angels) singing or playing instruments—but again, these are not portraits. Famous musicians typically included legendary figures—biblical characters such as Jubal of Old Testament fame, the "inventor" of music.

Our choices, and the availability of portraits, also have been affected by technological developments. Around the mid-nineteenth century, photography increasingly took over the function of portraiture, partly, at first, due to the public's fascination with this new medium. Kurt Blaukopf well describes what happened:

> Daguerre had taken the first photographic portraits, daguerrotypes, in 1839. Technical advances followed, and by the middle of the century the first portrait studios were being established—primarily in big cities, but soon, too, in smaller towns. The décor of these studios, and the style of the photographs, corresponded to the taste of the time: people in their Sunday best in the luxurious surroundings of the studio. (p. 11)

Thus we have many photographs of Brahms but few if any significant painted portraits. The same applies to Offenbach and others, though caricature continued to be a popular graphic medium, characterized by the distortion and humor that photography could not supply.

In the twentieth century the novelty of photography began to wear off, but the easy accessibility of the medium, and the need it satisfies for quick and inexpensive portraits, for publicity and other purposes, continue to supply us with far more photographic portraits, at the expense of painting and other artistic media.

Sometimes the existence or lack of a portrait tells us something about the composer himself. Consider, for example, Georges Bizet. There is a drawing of the twenty-five-year-old composer, not by a major artist. Bizet, born in 1838, had little success with his earlier works, including the opera *Les pêcheurs de perles* (1863) which soon was withdrawn. Only in the last year of his life did he receive substantial recognition—but even *Carmen* was not a success, with the public or critics, until after Bizet's death at the age of thirty-five. We can understand why no great painter gave us his portrait.

Finally, in some instances our choice was limited by our inability to obtain a good quality reproduction of a portrait, or to obtain permission to reproduce it. We may, of course, have overlooked some important portraits, and we would welcome comments from our readers about such omissions.

Some readers may be curious about other portraits of the composer in question, or about other musicians portrayed by the same artist. We have included such iconographic information in cases where it seemed specially relevant or was not readily accessible in English. Our extensive bibliography is intended to help readers with

further explorations of their own.

For each portrait in this volume we wanted to know: Who were the artists? What is the portrait's history? How, when, and where did artist and musician meet? Sometimes history has covered its tracks, but at other times, history has a story to tell. In many instances the portraits were done from life; that is, the musician sat, formally or informally, for the artist. In those circumstances we would assume that some personal interaction took place.

Collaborations between a well-known painter and a famous composer are apt to be well documented. For others, we have tried to discover the circumstances that led to the creation of a particular portrait, from life, posthumously, or at a distance. For asking our questions—what does the work tell us about the composer, about the artist?—we have been rewarded with a fascinating and colorful journey.

Introduction

Despite certain limitations in scope, portraiture is one of the most varied, changing, and interesting subjects in the visual arts. The human face has fascinated artists at least as far in the past as Old Kingdom Egypt. Since that time, different cultures have had remarkably varied conventions for portraying their citizens. Even though the Hellenistic Greeks and their Roman counterparts lived in much the same part of the world at the same time, the two civilizations developed dramatically different attitudes toward portraiture. While such differences have tended to disappear with increased exchange among cultures over the years, there is still a marked distinction at the end of the nineteenth century, for instance, in the ways Franz von Lenbach, a German, and Auguste Renoir, a Frenchman, represented the same subject, Richard Wagner.

These cultural distinctions, and the styles to which they give rise, are largely products of a people's history. Representation of the human face changes dramatically, say, between the thirteenth and fourteenth centuries in Gothic France. By contrast, period styles, such as the rococo, tend to eradicate distinctions between cultures, especially as practiced by less independent artists working within that style. Generally speaking, the stronger or more creative the artist, the more unique that artist's treatment of a given composer is likely to be.

The various cultural, historical, and stylistic differences reflected in a portrait also say a great deal about the subject and the fame or mystique—sometimes even the cult—that grew up around that individual. The rapport that occurs between composer and artist in the process of creating the portrait, however, is frequently difficult to ascertain and describe. All these variables, particularly the more impenetrable psychological ones, often come into play when great artists portray great composers. A portrait testifies to this complex interrelationship of history, geography, style, and psychology. Few situations can be more volatile and perhaps more productive than those that find two important artists together, one as subject, the other as creator. Fortunately, in the case of this volume, we have many of the visual records of those meetings which preserve, more or less, the appearance of the composers and provide a record of the artist's creative abilities.

The earliest composers' portraits are undoubtedly as old as the first representations of musicians, dating to Sumerian and Egyptian times. More frequently then than today, people who played music were often also those who composed it. Since the names of these court and temple musicians are unknown and their musical compositions have not survived, it is difficult to think of them as composers, especially in the fashion in which postmedieval Western culture has grown accustomed to identifying a particular composition with its creator.

Much the same can be said for the Greek world. Literature, of course, contains the names of gods, demigods, muses, and certainly mortals who either inspired or composed much music. Unfortunately virtually none of the fragments of that music that remain can be ascribed to any particular composer. Representations of mythological figures such as Orpheus, Apollo, Marsayas, and Polyhymnia abound, but these are not composers in the way that word is understood today. Indeed, we have pictures of them, but none that can be called true portraits.

It is difficult to find portraits, either imagined or done from life, of specific composers much before the fifteenth century. Extant illustrations of the Greek gods of music, such as Orpheus, are at best classically idealized conceptions of these immortal musicians, conveyed by artists well-schooled in representing the gods in human form. At the close of antiquity, artists who chose to represent angels, saints, and clerics of the new

Christian religion bestowed on these figures a debased form of classicism, carried over from the Hellenistic world. This variant of classicism was so abbreviated that it left figures virtually without distinguishing characteristics, either in the treatment of the body or of the face. This particular lack of identifying features is fully evident in the portrait of Pope Gregory the Great, part of a small ivory diptych from Monza Cathedral (Fig. 1). While most of the surrounding attributes are Christian, Gregory has been given both the pose and the simplified, abstract face of a ruler of the late Roman Empire. More by legend than by documented fact, Pope Gregory was said to be a composer, though his role was probably that of collecting and codifying the type of liturgical chants that bear his name. It is extremely doubtful that Gregory posed for this portrait. Still it is one of the earliest surviving representations of a "composer" done by an artist (who probably lived in the seventh century), contemporary enough with the Pope (c. 540–604) to have known something of his actual appearance on the basis of firsthand knowledge, from literature, or by word of mouth.

Created at least two centuries after the consular diptych showing Pope Gregory, the *King David* from the Paris Psalter, a product of a brilliant resurgence of classicism in the Byzantine world, portrays another religious leader and composer. Like Hellenistic representations of Orpheus, King David has been given such generalized, Greek characteristics that he seems little more than a youthful musician, with no unique or identifying facial features. This is only one among many representations of David dating from this period. The Old Testament composer-king was popular during Carolingian times and was often shown seated imperially, playing his lyre while surrounded by court musicians who join him on various medieval instruments. The image of the seated David, as the composer-king, derives from dual models: the enthroned Roman ruler and portraits of New Testament evangelists. Generally speaking, neither is more detailed in appearance than the Paris *David*.

The earliest painting of an actual composer, *Notker Balbulus*, probably created by a contemporary in the ninth or tenth century, also comes directly from the tradition of the seated evangelist figure. This is not without reason. One of the most important composers of sequence texts (a piece of sacred chant set syllabically with a Latin text), Notker also wrote stories, poetry, biography, and letters. It is thus as a writer that artists chose to portray him, though they most likely did not know that the pose of the seated evangelist, in which they represented him, was based on that reserved for Greek and Roman

Pope Gregory the Great depicted on portion of seventh-century ivory diptych, Treasury, Monza Cathedral

King David portrayed in the Paris Psalter (c. 900 A.D.), Bibliothèque Nationale, Paris

authors. In other words, Notker is shown not as an individual, but as a type, the thinking writer with head on hands and small, fixed eyes. Even though Notker was probably painted by one of his fellow monks, the artist, in keeping with medieval precedent, chose to ignore the famous musician's distinguishing physical characteristics, emphasizing instead those features—head and hands—which are the most important parts of the body for a writer.

In the five centuries that separate Notker from the Italian vocal writer, Francesco Landini, the type of pose adopted for the composer scarcely changes. The fifteenth-century portrait of Francesco, probably painted shortly after his

death, in the Squarcialupi Codex, shows the composer seated, playing a small, portable organ. The style of this Renaissance portrait, however, is much more contemporary than the pose and surroundings of the figure might otherwise indicate. The body, for instance, rendered with real weight, is seated rather convincingly. Another depiction of Francesco exists, this one full-length. It is found on his gravestone in the Basilica of San Lorenzo, Florence. Far more conservative in style, this image poses Francesco rigidly, his body so flat it seems essentially without form. These two studies of the composer come from a transitional period in which the conflict between the old and the new

11

The composer Notker Balbulus, ninth or tenth century manuscript illumination, Staatsarchiv, Zürich

earliest portrait of a composer done in oils. Van Eyck has also shown his subject from bust up, virtually without accompanying, perhaps distracting, artifacts. This, together with the use of oils, allows the artist to examine Gilles with previously unseen naturalism. The lines in his forehead and the wrinkles around his eyes are detailed with unsurpassed clarity. Likewise, the detached gaze gives some indication of the psychological disposition of the sitter.

Van Eyck's portrait was, indeed, ahead of its time. More than a century was required before easel painting, done in oils, became the standard technique for rendering composers' portraits. For the remainder of the fifteenth century, paintings of composers were largely restricted to manuscript form. The reasons for this are, at root, both social and economic. Composers did not yet possess either sufficient social status or financial means to command portraits of stature. The more important fifteenth-century composers were court musicians. As such, they rarely served as portrait subjects on panel or canvas, a type of painting usually reserved for more prominent citizens.

While composers might not be of sufficient rank for treatment as the exclusive subject of painting, their status was great enough for portrayal more frequently than their predecessors, though in miniature form. In *Le Champion des dames,* Gilles Binchois is again presented, this time with his contemporary Guillaume Dufay, each no taller than two inches in the original. In the text below the illumination, Martin LeFranc, author of *Le Champion,* wrote of these two Flemish composers:

Tapissier, Carmen, Cesaris
In recent times well did sing
They were the wonder of all Paris....
[Dufay and Binchois] have found a newer
    way
Of making fresh bright concordance
In public music and in private songs
With *Fict,* rests and mutation.

For all their contributions, however, Binchois and Dufay still remain indistinguishable in their facial characteristics. Only the type and color of their clothing, and the instruments that accompany them—Binchois a lyre and Dufay an organetto—differentiate one composer from the other.

Portraits of two other Flemish composers of the early Renaissance come down to us in small-scale, manuscript format: Johannes Martini, composer at the court of the d'Este family in Ferrara; and the better-known Josquin Desprez. Neither representation is authoritative. The miniature bust portrait, long said to be that of

in the visual arts clearly parallels the position occupied by Francesco's songs in the history of music. The gravestone looks back toward the fourteenth century while the manuscript illumination points the way toward the new Renaissance style of the fifteenth century.

The novelty and strength of this new, more naturalistic way of painting can be fully seen in the portrait of Gilles Binchois by the Flemish painter, Jan van Eyck. An inscription on the illusionistic ledge below the figure dates the portrait to 1432. While we do not know conclusively that it is Gilles behind the parapet in this work, Erwin Panofsky has made a strong case for identification of the sitter as the well-known Burgundian composer. The painting is justly famous. If it is Gilles, or indeed any other writer of music at the court of Philip the Good, then it constitutes the

Fifteenth-century portrait of Francesco Landini in the Squarcialupi Codex, Biblioteca Medicea Laurenziana, Florence

The Flemish composer Gilles Binchois (?) by Jan van Eyck (1432), oil, The National Gallery, London

Johannes Martini (c. 1490), may not in fact be a painting of the d'Este court composer. Likewise, the woodcut of Desprez was done in 1611, almost two centuries after the composer's death. Despite their growing fame, these composers of the early Renaissance still were not, on the whole, represented with either the skill or on the scale accorded many rulers, clerics, or merchants of the day.

The sixteenth century is a period of transition in the evolving portrait of the composer. At the beginning of the century, these images are still found in manuscript form. By its end, artists begin to concentrate their attentions more specifically on their musical counterparts' appearance and, increasingly, on their inner character. There is a marvelously instructive miniature, *Johannes Ockeghem and His Cantors*, found in the *Recuel de chants royaux* (c. 1530). This painting, which measures approximately thirty by twenty centimeters, has not only grown in size over its predecessors, but it is clearly a scene, not a portrait. Painted some thirty years after his death, the miniature depicts Ockeghem standing in the foreground, directing his choir while following music on a lectern to his left. The

Binchois and Guillaume Dufay, fifteenth-century illumination in Martin LeFranc, Le Champion des dames, *Bibliothèque Nationale, Paris*

Johannes Ockeghem and His Cantors *(c. 1530),
Bibliothèque Nationale, Paris*

anonymous artist responsible for this composition conceived something broader in scope than an individual's portrait. Instead, he chose to show his subject in surroundings that could be identified with him.

Generally speaking, this expanded version is preferred by artists of the sixteenth century for paintings that include composers' portraits, either posthumous or from life, in manuscript or on panel. Not only Ockeghem, but Heinrich Isaac, Ludwig Senfl, and Roland de Lassus are also shown in the context of making music. Undoubtedly the Renaissance emphasis on credible pictorial space is responsible, in part, for this phenomenon, as is the waning importance of the illuminated manuscript. Certainly, the growing fame and influence of great writers of music were significant in the development of individual easel portraits of composers, usually done on canvas. These occur very sporadically in the late Renaissance, but are painted with increasing persuasiveness at the beginning of the baroque. It is here, at this important watershed between the Renaissance and the baroque, between illustrations of composers and true portraits of them, that our survey of great composers' portraits appropriately begins.

14

PORTRAITS

Martin Luther

The visual image we have of Martin Luther (1483–1546) today depends on Lucas Cranach's portraits of the religious reformer. Cranach painted Luther in at least seven different versions. In addition, copies, executed for the most part by the master's extensive workshop, are numerous. To be sure, Cranach did not treat Luther so frequently in both paintings and prints because of the latter's musical talents, which were many. Instead, the German painter represented Luther as a controversial historical and religious figure whose notoriety and popularity grew to vast proportions in the Germany of his day. Cranach also painted Luther repeatedly because the two were extremely close friends.

In the twelve years that elapsed between the earliest of Cranach's portraits of Luther and that represented here, the subject grew from a gaunt, emaciated monk to a member of the Saxon bourgeoisie. His face became fuller, a feature emphasized by Cranach's use of sinuous line and mildly mannered modeling. Luther appears uncomfortable in this portrait. His shoulders join the frame at slightly different heights, and he holds his head at an awkward angle to his body. These various peculiarities give the painting a curious vitality, which is reinforced by the penetrating gaze that was one of the subject's most telling attributes in life.

After training with his father and spending three years in Vienna, Lucas Cranach (1472–1553) was called to serve the Elector Frederick the Wise of Saxony at his court in Wittenberg in 1504. Until the time of his death, almost fifty years later, Cranach served Frederick and his successors. By 1517, when he first painted Luther, Cranach had become a wealthy, established, and important citizen of Wittenberg. In 1520, Frederick the Wise granted the painter, who already doubled as wine merchant, an apothecary shop, a privilege which carried with it residence in one of the town's magnificent houses. In 1519, Cranach also served as the treasurer to the city council. He held the position of town counselor at least six separate times, and was chosen mayor of the city from 1537 to 1544. Tax records reveal Cranach to be one of the two wealthiest landowners in town.

The relationship between the two men is among the closest between composer and artist recounted in this book. We cannot be certain when the two first met, but since both were leading citizens of Wittenberg, it might have been as early as 1508 when Luther began to teach at the university there. As criticism against the young dissident grew, so did Luther's friendship with Cranach. In 1520, Luther stood as godfather to the artist's daughter, Anna. When Luther refused to recant at the Diet of Worms in 1521 and was spirited off to protective safety in the Wartburg (seat of the landgraves of Thuringia) by the Elector, Frederick, Cranach became the first Wittenberger taken into the fleeing radical's confidence. Cranach painted Luther as a landowner, the *Junker Jörg,* when the latter appeared in Wittenberg in disguise for three days in December 1521.

Perhaps the most intriguing episode in this friendship began in 1523, the year after Luther returned to Wittenberg from the Wartburg. Luther had helped engineer the escape of nine Augustinian nuns from captivity in the convent at Nimbschen, and placed one of them, Katharina von Bora, in the magnificent house of the town's apothecary, Lucas Cranach. There she became like a daughter of the house. After trying to marry Katharina to two of his friends, Luther married the former nun himself in 1525. Cranach and his wife represented Katharina's family at the wedding, and, the next year, the painter became godfather to Luther's first son, Johannes. The image of Luther represented here, first painted in 1529, is a version of a dual portrait with his wife (not shown) in the pendant facing him.

Luther began his activity as a composer during the 1520s. In addition to his other talents, Luther was a gifted musician. He played both lute and flute and seems to have possessed a soft, lyric tenor voice. In choirs, he sang Gregorian chants, masses, and motets, and learned the work of Josquin and Senfl on his fateful trip to Rome, 1510–11.

In music, Luther's greatest concern was to provide hymns to be sung by the congregation during worship. Early twentieth-century academicians denied Luther credit for most of the church music attributed to him by his contemporaries. Recent scholarship, however, credits more than thirty-five hymns to the theologian-composer, particularly those from the Wittenberg hymnals. The majority of these date to 1523 and 1524, the time when his friendship with Cranach was closest. In addition, Luther wrote chants for the church, revised the Latin Mass, and wrote a new vernacular German Mass. As was common among German *Meistersinger,* Luther would have been responsible for both verse and music in his religious works. His verses were simple and direct; his melodies, borrowed from sources as varied as plain song and folk tunes, possessed many of the same qualities.

Martin Luther *by Lucas Cranach the Elder (1529), oil on panel, 37.5 × 23.5 cm, Uffizi Gallery, Florence*

17

John Bull

This fascinating portrait of John Bull (?1562–1628), the noted English virginalist and keyboard composer, was painted by an anonymous limner (a painter of portraits in miniature) at the height of the Elizabethan period, when the Renaissance was still gathering strength in England. No small portion of the work's importance rests on its place in the development of portraiture in Renaissance England. On one hand, the *Bull* is a stunning example of the portrait artist's growing success at working with relatively recent technical innovations, painting with oils on panel (in this case, set off by a distinguished, inscribed frame). On the other, its style still shows some of the influences of manuscript illumination. Portraiture, either in the form of miniatures or full-scale studies, replaced illumination as the principal form of painting in sixteenth-century England.

Here, John Bull exists in a flat, spaceless world that is the trademark of sixteenth- and seventeenth-century British portraiture (later exported to North America). Only minimal interest in volume is to be found in areas such as the shading of the cheeks and the rear of the sitter's fur stole, beneath which there is only the slightest suggestion of a body. Despite the skull and hourglass to the left rear and the inscription across from it, the background too is perfectly flat. Devoid of most spatial rendering, the painting preserves Bull's features in changeless, iconic form, unaffected by the ephemeral qualities of light, shading, or atmosphere.

The painting can be securely dated from the inscription in the upper right corner, *"An Aetatis Svae 27, 1589."* Shown at age twenty-seven, Bull was a rapidly rising young musician and composer at the court of Elizabeth I. Three years earlier he had been appointed a Gentleman of the Chapel Royal, in which capacity he served well into the reign of James I. By 1589 he had also been awarded a doctorate of music from Cambridge.

Of interest equal to the inscription is its shadowy counterpart, a lightly printed skull and bone atop an hourglass to the right of Bull's head. Usually a reminder of the passing of time and the proximity of death, the eerie device has more recently been taken as an indication of Bull's interest in alchemy, in which skull and hourglass stood as talismans of victory over mortality. This fascination with alchemic and neo-Platonic sciences carried over to Bull's own work, and may be found in both visual and musical form in his puzzle canon, *Sphera mundi.*

The noted severity of Bull's compositional style comes through in the demeanor of the sitter and the paucity of his surroundings. Bodyless, fixed immovably against the flat background, Bull peers beyond the frame of the painting with sharp, penetrating eyes. It is not difficult to make a psychological reading of the portrait, suggesting that the unknown artist was a fairly astute judge of character. The keen intellect displayed in Bull's canons can be seen in the intelligence and composure of his features. On the other hand, the splendor of his garments, especially the stole and detailed collar, give visual evidence of a sensuality on the part of the subject. This inclination toward gratification of the senses would later precipitate the loss of significant court appointments for adulterous liaisons on at least two separate occasions, the last (recorded) of which forced him to flee the patronage of James I to the Netherlands, where he would spend the remaining fifteen years of his life.

Perhaps the author of the inscription on the painting's frame saw this in the young musician's personality and wrote:

> The Bull by force
> In field doth Raigne
> But Bull by Skill
> Good will doth Gayne.

John Bull, *anonymous (1589), oil on panel, Heather Professor of Music, Oxford University*

Text on frame:
The Bull by force

AN ATATIS SVÆ 27
1589

In field doth Raigne

But Bull by Skill

Good will doth Gayne

Claudio Monteverdi

As with the likenesses of many other seventeenth- and eighteenth-century composers, the painter of our portrait of Claudio Monteverdi (1567–1643), one of the earliest composers of opera, is not known for certain. The story behind the probable identity of the artist is a long, interesting one.

The painting illustrated here in black and white first came into the collection of the Ferdinandeum in Innsbruck in 1880 and is now thought to be a copy of the original. When it was acquired, the Ferdinandeum painting was thought to be a portrait of Monteverdi's famous precursor, Giovanni Palestrina, done by the late mannerist painter G. B. Moroni. In 1937, a similarity was noted between the Ferdinandeum painting and an engraving of Monteverdi, done by a Venetian artist (J. Decini?) in 1644, the year after the composer's death. The facial features in both the painting and the engraving were remarkably similar. Both men possess the same long faces, hairlines, aquiline features, and penetrating eyes. Then, in 1955, Luisa Mortari identified the portrait's artist as Bernardo Strozzi (1581–1644), based on the existence of another portrait of Monteverdi by Strozzi, which was on display in Venice in the latter half of the seventeenth century.

In 1977 Mortari published the portrait of Monteverdi shown here in color, which now resides in the Gesellschaft der Musikfreunde in Vienna. A poem by the famous Venetian writer, Giulio Strozzi, has been inscribed beneath the book in the portrait's lower right-hand corner. The inscription reads:

> Painted by the famous Abbot Bernardo Strozzi,
> I am called Claudio of the green mountain [Monteverdi].
> Oh, ancient one, detach your powerful image from the canvas underneath,
> Aeson rejected the cure which you, Medea, carried out.

Based on this inscription, the Vienna painting is now thought to be the original Monteverdi and the portrait in the Ferdinandeum a copy. In 1635, Bernardo also painted a portrait of the poet Giulio Strozzi (Ashmolean Museum, Oxford) who wrote the inscription for the Vienna *Monteverdi*.

The pose chosen by Bernardo Strozzi for his subject is animated, even by the standards of the early baroque (a feature tacitly acknowledged in the third line of the inscription). Perhaps during his later years, Strozzi returned to the style of his youth, mannerism, which favored more complicated poses, elongated figures, and dramatic lighting. In both portraits, Monteverdi sits forward boldly, his arms circling in front of him so that his hands rest on an unidentified musical manuscript. His head angles forcefully to the side as he stares in a direct way beyond the canvas. The dynamic contrast between light and dark, which Strozzi undoubtedly learned from followers of Caravaggio, draws attention to head and hands. An arbitrary diagonal patch of light intersects the strong lines of the arms and upper body. The success of these various pictorial dynamics may well have inspired the poet Giulio Strozzi, in the painting's inscription, to summon Monteverdi from the canvas.

The painting dates toward the end of Monteverdi's life when both he and Strozzi occupied positions of prominence in their respective artistic traditions, music and painting, in Venice. That means the portrait would have been executed between 1630, about the time Strozzi is thought to have arrived in the city, and 1643, the year of Monteverdi's death (Strozzi would follow him one year later). From his native Genoa, where he had been strongly influenced by Van Dyck and Rubens, Strozzi would bring both the quiet drama of the baroque and a new spirit of contained emotion to the tradition of portraiture in Venice.

For his part, Monteverdi had moved to Venice

Monteverdi by Bernardo Strozzi, now considered a copy of the original. Tiroler Landesmuseum, Innsbruck

almost twenty years earlier than Strozzi, in 1613, to serve as chapelmaster there. Soon after the first public opera house was opened in the city in 1637, he would embark on two of the most significant operas of his career: *Il ritorno d'Ulisse in patria* (1640) and *L'incoronazione di Poppea* (1642). In both operas, especially the more seamless, lavish *L'incoronazione,* there is an increased understanding and deepening of emotional content similar to that witnessed in the portraits of Strozzi's last years. It is thus fitting that Monteverdi and Strozzi should find themselves involved in making a portrait, one of the most psychologically penetrating of human endeavors, in the city of Venice, a metropolis native to neither of them.

21

Barbara Strozzi

As it is currently displayed in Dresden, our painting of Barbara Strozzi bears the title *Female Musician with a Viola da Gamba*. It was first shown in the United States as part of a traveling exhibition, the Splendor of Dresden, in 1978. As a consequence of that exhibition, David and Ellen Rosand proposed that the subject is not an anonymous female musician, but rather the baroque singer and composer, Barbara Strozzi (1619–1664?).

Unfortunately this painting cannot be securely dated. If indeed Barbara Strozzi is the subject, Bernardo Strozzi (1581–1644) would have painted her toward the end of his life, when he was in Venice. The date of his arrival there is uncertain, sometime between 1630 and 1635. This latter date is inscribed on a portrait Bernardo painted of Giulio Strozzi (Ashmolean Museum, Oxford, 1635), and provides the latest possible date for the painter's advent in that city.

Clearly, the *Female Musician* preserves the influence of Caravaggio's strong contrasts of light against a dark ground, an approach which Bernardo Strozzi favored toward the middle of his life, when he was still in his native Genoa. The more lively colors and the spontaneous brushwork reflect aspects of the artistic tradition Strozzi would have learned in Venice from that city's great painters of the previous century: Titian, Veronese, Tintoretto. Like so many of his fellow baroque artists, Strozzi absorbed and modified the styles of new regions in which he traveled.

So far as we know, Barbara Strozzi was no relation to the painter of the portrait. There is, however, an interesting historical connection between the two families: the portrait Bernardo painted of Giulio Strozzi. The latter was Barbara's father by adoption and perhaps her biological father. A second, looser connection exists in the inscription Giulio supplied for Bernardo's portrait of Claudio Monteverdi (see pp. 20f.).

Giulio Strozzi was a leading figure in the intellectual and cultural life of early seventeenth-century Venice. A poet and dramatist, he also played an active role in the city's musical circles, supplying libretti for two operas by Monteverdi and one by Cavalli. He provided texts for a variety of different vocal pieces, including some for his "elective" daughter's first book of madrigals (1644). Giulio himself was a member of the famous *Accademia degli Incogniti*, and inaugurated three academies. One, the *Accademia degli Unisoni*, was designed in large part as a showcase for Barbara's musical talents. Here she served as mistress of ceremonies and sang musical interludes. For whatever reason, perhaps the lightness of her voice, it appears she never sang in any productions staged in that city's growing number of opera houses.

If this painting indeed features the composer, it may corroborate a number of satires which attacked both the reputation of the *Accademia degli Unisoni* and its principal entertainer. The flowers in the figure's hair suggested to David and Ellen Rosand an allegorical identification with Flora, the Roman goddess of flowers, who, in this particular manifestation, may also be Flora *meretrice*, the patroness of courtesans. The subject herself holds a viola da gamba. A violin lies on the table below the open manuscript of a duet, both devices serving, in sixteenth- and seventeenth-century art, to suggest the anticipated presence of a second player. Likewise her plunging décolleté and open gaze seem to invite participation. Perhaps Bernardo Strozzi knew Barbara Strozzi's music, the lyricism of which was in part designed to establish direct contact with her audiences.

As one might expect from a composer who was also a singer, all eight published volumes of Strozzi's music are cantatas and arias for solo voice and basso continuo. All but one of the songs in them are secular. Their principal subject is the expression of love—in particular, feelings of unrequited love.

Published over a twenty-year period, her compositions demonstrate remarkable development. This is especially true in the arias which, in their early form, manifest a simple, repeated melodic structure from stanza to stanza. By the end of her career, her arias display much greater complexity, variety, and freedom.

These arias were written primarily with the composer in mind; she probably would have accompanied herself on the lute while singing them. She wrote all but two for her voice type, soprano. For the most part they were intended for simple gatherings, such as those sponsored by the *Accademia degli Unisoni*. Strozzi herself supervised her compositions' publication. Thus, rather than dismiss her songs as casual entertainment for limited performance by their composer, she thought enough of her compositions to foster their dissemination and preservation.

Female Musician with a Viola da Gamba by Bernardo Strozzi (c.1640), oil on canvas, 126 × 99 cm, Gemäldegalerie Alte Meister, Staatliche Kunstsammlungen Dresden

Heinrich Schütz

A sensitive, compelling *Portrait of a Man with a Sheet of Music*, perhaps painted by Rembrandt (1606–1669), hangs in the Corcoran Gallery in Washington, D.C. The present title of the painting derives from the scroll of paper, containing musical notation, held in the sitter's left hand. In portraits such as this, Rembrandt usually did not devote more attention to his subjects' faces, or to their psyches, than his viewers could take in at a glance. In this sense his *Man with a Sheet of Music* is unusual. It is a bust-length portrait, with the subject pushed forward to create a feeling of intimacy. The artist focuses attention on the composer's kindly face, not on details of his apparel. In part, he succeeds in this through his maturing *chiaroscuro*, the contrast between light and dark. Here, his interest in light is still relatively naturalistic when compared to his later portraits, yet light adds warmth that radiates from the composer's face.

As early as 1937, Bruno Maerker suggested that the Corcoran Rembrandt may, indeed, be a painting of the great German composer Heinrich Schütz (1585–1672). When compared to known portraits of Schütz, the musician in *Man with a Sheet of Music* also has the same wrinkled brow, heavy eyelids and expressive eyes, arched nose, sensitive lips, protruding jaw, and distinctive beard.

Unfortunately no documents exist to link Schütz with the Corcoran portrait. Furthermore, Rembrandt never left the Netherlands in his life, and Schütz's presence in that country has never been established. These circumstances, plus the portrait's lack of volume and attention to detail, have led S. H. Levie and a team of Dutch scholars, the Rembrandt Research Project, to question Rembrandt's authorship of the *Man with a Sheet of Music*. Their findings have been recently published in *A Corpus of Rembrandt Paintings*.

From as early as 1618, Schütz served as chapelmaster to Elector Johann Georg I of Saxony where the great German composer's duties included providing music, both sacred and secular, for court. After spending the year 1629 in Italy, where he published his *Symphoniae sacrae*, Op. 6, Schütz returned to Dresden. Between 1629 and the year of his departure for Denmark, 1633, Schütz composed little music that has been preserved, in part because of the Thirty Years' War. Saxony, which had remained neutral in that disastrous religious conflict, formed an alliance with Gustavus Adolphus of Sweden in 1631. Because the Elector of Saxony diverted money to the military effort, music at court suffered.

It was under these circumstances that Schütz may have sat for Rembrandt in Amsterdam in 1633. The chapelmaster received a letter inviting him to Copenhagen to direct music for the marriage of Prince Christian of Denmark to Johann Georg's daughter, Magdalena Sibylla. We do not know precisely when Schütz left for Copenhagen, possibly as early as July 1633. He spent at least two months in the fall of that year in Hamburg before traveling on to the Danish Court. Perhaps while in Hamburg, or in the two months that preceded his stay there, he could have visited Amsterdam. There certainly was much of musical interest in that city to attract the great German composer. The noted organ maker, composer, and teacher, Jan Sweelinck, was survived by his son, Jan, who carried on his father's tradition. There was also a *collegium musicum* and a circle of the city's leading intellectuals who were greatly interested in music.

Two years before painting the *Man with a Sheet of Music*, Rembrandt had established himself in Amsterdam, where he developed a growing reputation as a portrait painter. Members of that city's merchant and upper classes sought out the artist, and for good reason. Rembrandt had cultivated a technique in the use of oils which allowed him to depict, with uncanny accuracy, the finery worn by many of his sitters. Elements of Dutch costume—especially jewelry, embroidery, lace collars and cuffs—came to life in his portraits. It may seem strange to emphasize these particular features of dress, but Rembrandt's subjects paid increasing sums for the artist's ability to represent the material values to which many of them had dedicated their lives.

Rembrandt and Schütz could have been introduced by common friends in Amsterdam. More to the point, Rembrandt was a devoted student of the Old Testament. He also took a profound interest in subjects that featured intellectual pursuits—music, literature, and philosophy among them. Any artist who could paint Saul weeping to music composed by David could appreciate the talents of Heinrich Schütz. Rarely in Rembrandt's early portraits (even in his self-portraits) are his sitters rendered with the empathy that is found in the melting features of Rembrandt's *Man with a Sheet of Music*. His large, liquid eyes and delicate lips radiate the more passionate, expressive qualities that characterize Schütz's early music.

Portrait of a Man with a
Sheet of Music *by
Rembrandt van Rijn (?)
(1633), oil on panel, 64 ×
45.5 cm, The Corcoran
Gallery of Art,
Washington, D.C.*

Jean-Baptiste Lully

During the reign of Louis XIV, France saw one of the greatest flourishings of the arts in Europe, sponsored and actively furthered by the king.

The composer who came to be most closely involved in this flourishing of music and dance at court, in Versailles and Paris, was an Italian, born in Florence as Giovanni Battista Lulli (1632–1687). He came to France as a boy of fourteen; as Jean-Baptiste Lully he became the leading French composer of the seventeenth century. Like the king, he was a dancer and guitar player, though his talents as a violinist contributed more to his success at court. In 1653 we find him composing for the king, chiefly ballet music. By 1661 he had risen to the position of leader (*surintendant*) and soon was given the title of *maître de la musique de la famille royale*.

Fully supported by the monarch, Lully directed everything: the work of assistant composers and copyists, of ballet masters, costume and set designers, of machinists—even the work of his librettist.

Lully also had a talent for diplomacy, for making a crucial move at the right time. He knew just when to approach the king with his not-very-veiled request to become his secretary—a very prestigious appointment which was granted and which raised the incumbent to the ranks of the nobility.

This kind of political finesse, coupled with a gift for behind-the-scenes maneuvering, in no way diminishes Lully's accomplishments as a composer. It is no small part of his achievement that, during his time and into the eighteenth century, French music, and especially French opera, was able to maintain a high degree of independence from Italian music. Italian *maestri* and Italian music set the tone and ruled the roost virtually everywhere else in Europe and in the New World.

This brings us to the Lully portrait by Mignard, generally considered the best. It has become well known through the engraving by Jean-Louis Roullet, based on the painting. The engraving (perhaps also the painting) must have been made after 1680 because its caption refers to the composer as *Secrétaire du Roy*. (Only in the second place does it list his musical title!) This was the decade of Lully's greatest successes, which might be seen to justify not only the formality of the portrait but also the laudatory verses which appear under the engraving. Lully's glory, we are told, has replaced (or extinguished) that of Orpheus; Lully's, not Orpheus', lyre (the symbol of instrumental music) and voice are charming "the greatest of Kings."

Lully's posture and mien are rigid and serious, in the best tradition of seventeenth-century portraits of distinguished personages. He holds a music scroll in his right hand—the emblem of his profession. Actually, such a roll of music manuscript traditionally served in lieu of a baton, especially for conducting church music, until the early nineteenth century. In opera, a long staff, rather than a short baton as we know it, served the director to mark time, audibly, by pounding on the floor. One of the most widely known facts about Lully has to do with his use of such a staff: he hit his foot, leading to injury, blood poisoning, and death.

The authorship of our painting is not entirely certain, largely because the Mignard family included a number of painters, all listed in Thieme-Becker's *Lexicon*. The Lully portrait has been attributed to several of them, including Pierre Mignard (1612–1695). We know that he lived for more than twenty years in Rome where he painted the portraits of three popes and many members of the aristocracy. In 1657 he returned to France, by command of the king, and became a successful portraitist there, especially after the death of Charles Le Brun, his rival, who had been painter to the king. Others consider Pierre Mignard the Younger (1640–1725) to have executed the Lully portrait. Paul Mignard the Younger (1639–1691), however, is the most likely painter; his name (as Paulus Mignard) appears at the bottom of the Roullet engraving. He became a member of the Académie Royale in 1672.

Jean-Baptiste Lully, engraving by Jean-Louis Roullet, based on the portrait by Paul Mignard

Jean-Baptiste Lully *by [Paul?] Mignard (c. 1680), oil on canvas, 66 × 56 cm (oval), Musée Condé, Chantilly*

Arcangelo Corelli

Not much is known about the early life of Arcangelo Corelli (1653–1713), whom we see here, portrayed as a mature artist. By 1666 he had gone to Bologna, then a flourishing center of instrumental music. He must have distinguished himself there, for soon (1670) he was admitted to the prestigious *Accademia Filharmonica* of that city. His rise to international fame occurred after he settled in Rome around 1675.

The city's nobility, including some princes of the church, supported a vigorous musical life. Several Roman cardinals maintained private house orchestras; Corelli participated in several of them as violinist-director. Handel and Alessandro Scarlatti were among the well-known composers also frequenting these circles.

By 1679 Corelli had entered the services of Queen Christina of Sweden (who had given up her throne and converted to Catholicism), one of the most active patrons of music in the Eternal City. Corelli dedicated his first published set of trio sonatas to her in 1681. His prowess as a violinist and composer of string music had begun to establish his international reputation.

Corelli's increasing fame attracted violin students from Italy and abroad; his (relatively few) sets of sonatas and concerti grossi were published during his lifetime and frequently reprinted in many countries. They still form part of the basic repertory of violinists and chamber orchestras, the "Christmas Concerto" being a perennial favorite.

The only well-known Corelli portrait was painted by Hugh Howard (b. Dublin, 1675; d. London, 1737 or 1738). Several versions of the painting exist, as well as engravings based on it. Marc Pincherle (*Corelli,* 200–201) dates it between 1697 and 1700, one engraving having been published in 1704. Howard had traveled in Holland and Italy and studied for some years in Rome. He must have returned to Ireland soon after having painted Corelli; he later settled in London.

In his *General History of the Science and Practice of Music,* first published in 1776, Sir John Hawkins has much to say about Corelli and this portrait.

During the residence of Corelli in Rome, many persons were ambitious of becoming his disciples, and learning the practice on the violin from the greatest master of the instrument the world had then heard of. Of these it is said that the late Lord Edgecumbe was one; and that the fine mezzotinto print of Corelli by Smith, was scraped [engraved] from a picture painted by Mr. Hugh Howard at Rome for that nobleman. (vol. 2, 675–676)

In a footnote Hawkins elaborates:

This picture was painted between 1697 and 1700, for in that interval it appears that Mr. Howard was abroad.... That Corelli sat to Mr. Howard is certain, for in the print after it is this inscription: "H. Howard ad vivum pinxit."

Corelli, Hawkins continues,

is said to have been remarkable for the mildness of his temper and the modesty of his deportment; the lineaments of his countenance, as represented in his portrait, seem to bespeak as much; nevertheless he was not insensible to the respect due to his skill and exquisite performance.

Hawkins also relates several anecdotes about the "plainness of his garb" and about his humor. While Hawkins describes the composer as benign and gentle (as if to honor his first name, Arcangelo), Pincherle saw Corelli's expression in the portrait as animated and resolute: "All the features of his face seem to denote decision." Observers also reported that while performing, Corelli could become quite agitated, showing great emotion—behavior that was and is quite compatible with an otherwise gentle and modest personality.

Though our portrait is unsigned, it is fairly certain that it is the Howard painting which had been lost for some time (Marx).

Arcangelo Corelli by Hugh Howard (c. 1700), oil on paper mounted on board, 34.6 × 26.4 cm, Faculty of Music, Oxford University

29

Henry Purcell

It is perhaps no mistake that John Closterman (1660–1711) began his career in England as a painter who specialized in rendering drapery. The representation of lavish, in some cases implausible, drapes was nothing new there. With the work of Rubens and Van Dyck it had become a staple feature in portraits of British aristocracy. Here Closterman has draped Henry Purcell (1659–1695) in voluminous contrasting silks that only vaguely suggest functional articles of apparel. Loose, unlikely folds in the cloth display the artist's skill at handling the reflection of light off brilliantly reflective surfaces, a trademark of baroque portraiture.

The oval format of the portrait was also a standard seventeenth-century device, used frequently by Sir Peter Lely and Sir Godfrey Kneller, leading portraitists in England at the end of the baroque. Kneller, especially, preferred the oval portrait, with more fancifully rendered drapery, for portraits of the British intellectuals John Locke, Sir Isaac Newton, Samuel Pepys, and Alexander Pope.

The writing of excellent music by native composers thrived in Renaissance and baroque England; composers John Blow, John Bull, William Byrd, Thomas Morley, Thomas Weelkes, and Henry Purcell come immediately to mind.

The last named of these, Henry Purcell, lived only until age thirty-six. In that short time, he studied with John Blow and only slightly later served in rapid succession as organist of Westminster Abbey, then the Royal Chapel. Working well within the British tradition of vocal music, he wrote songs, choral works, court cantatas, and music for the theater. He branched out to instrumental music, and also created something of a rarity in England until the twentieth century, a British opera of great beauty and enduring appeal. His *Dido and Aeneas* is one of the few baroque operas still performed with some regularity today.

Music by English composers flourished in England during late sixteenth century and into the seventeeth; the same is not necessarily the case with painting. While Holbein, Rubens, and Van Dyck all visited the Sceptered Isle, painters approaching the stature of these foreigners were not to rise from British stock until the nineteenth century. The most popular form of painting through the baroque in England was the portrait. The British aristocracy had a penchant for having themselves painted. Curiously, many of the artists responsible for these Renaissance and baroque portraits were northern European by birth and often by training.

Like Hans Holbein and Godfrey Kneller, John Closterman came from German-speaking north central Europe. By the age of twenty-one he had settled in London, becoming a specialist at painting drapery for the English portraitist John Riley, who died in 1691. Even though Closterman had left his master eight years earlier, he quickly took over Riley's practice, painting such notable subjects as Queen Anne; her husband George, Prince of Denmark; John Dryden; Grinling Gibbons; John Locke; the Duke of Marlborough; and Queen Mary. Closterman's reputation has grown considerably since 1981 when the National Portrait Gallery devoted an exhibition and accompanying catalog to his work.

In matters relating to portraits of Henry Purcell, there is a strong connection between Closterman and Godfrey Kneller. In addition to the portrait pictured here, the National Portrait Gallery also has a chalk drawing of Purcell. Formerly, it was attributed to Kneller, and said to be the only portrait of Purcell done from life. Closterman's oil portrait is traditionally held to have been painted after Purcell's death. The angle of the head, the direction of the eyes, the silhouette of the nose, and especially the lines of the mouth are remarkably similar in both representations. Indeed, both painting and drawing are now attributed to Closterman.

The composer's final year was indeed a busy one, during which he worked primarily for the London theater, creating the music for *The Tempest* and *The Indian Queen*, and no fewer than six other plays. The portraitist inscribed his painting "*Henricus Purcell, Aetat: Svae 37. 95.*" This indicates the painting was done in 1695, the year of Purcell's early death of an unknown illness.

Henry Purcell by John Closterman (1695), oil on canvas, 73.7 × 61 cm, National Portrait Gallery, London

31

Antonio Vivaldi

That determined and headstrong look is much more in line with Vivaldi's character than the unctuous smile of the academic portraits.
MARC PINCHERLE

It is often an indication of popularity (and of a certain kind of success) if someone in the public eye has become the subject of caricatures. This applies as much to artists as to politicians; among composers, Paganini, Berlioz, Liszt, and especially Wagner are cases in point.

Eighteenth-century musicians supply fewer examples, though Handel's fame is thus documented (see p. 38). Another instance is that of the castrato Farinelli who sang in Handel's operas and whose fame was international.

Antonio Vivaldi (1678–1741) also was widely celebrated in his day, both as composer and violinist. He was far better known than J. S. Bach, his contemporary, partly because he was prominently involved in the remarkable musical life of a remarkable city: Venice.

Before he began teaching at one of the famed Venetian conservatories, Vivaldi had taken religious orders; because of this and the color of his hair, he was known as *il prete rosso*—the red priest.

Vivaldi must have been a musician of tremendous energies. He concertized extensively throughout Italy and abroad and composed hundreds of major works, usually at breakneck speed. A French observer described him in 1739: "He is an old man who composes furiously and prodigiously. I have heard him . . . compose a concerto with all its parts more quickly than a copyist could copy it" (Pincherle, 51).

Vivaldi's concertos (he wrote well over 400) remain his best-known works today. They feature virtually all instruments in use at the time, including mandolin, lute, piccolo, viola d'amore, and recorder. Among the violin concertos those of Op. 8, "The Seasons," enjoy greatest popularity today.

Obviously Vivaldi was hard-working and fast-working, not only as a composer but also as the manager, producer, organizer, and supervisor of all aspects of opera performances. Benedetto Marcello's famous satire on operatic practices of his time (*Il teatro alla moda*, Venice, 1720) hints at Vivaldi's popularity, if not notoriety, by several references on the title page: the engraving of an angel, wearing a priest's hat and playing the violin, no doubt suggests our composer, as does the name of the alleged printer: ALDIVIVA.

Few portraits of Vivaldi survive. That by François Morellon de la Cave dates from 1725. An engraving based on Cave's painting has often been reproduced, as in John Hawkins' *General History of . . . Music* (1776). Vivaldi scholars doubt that it was done from life; it is rather formal and does not reflect what we know of the composer's personality. For a realistic representation we turn to the sketch by Pier Leone Ghezzi (1674–1755). It is the only authenticated portrait, carrying the caption: "Il prete rosso Compositor di Musica che fece L'Opera a Capranica del 1723" (. . . who produced the opera at the Capranica Theater [in Rome] in 1723). Vivaldi's *Ercole sul Termodonte* was given there in January 1723.

Ghezzi was a painter in his own right, of sufficient stature to have done some frescoes in the Vatican and paintings in various Roman churches. But he is remembered chiefly for his realistic caricatures of contemporaries, famous or not. He drew literally hundreds of them, representing Romans from all walks of life, in full-length portraits or profiles. Many have captions in his own hand, such as our Vivaldi portrait (not shown).

Musicians figure prominently: Ghezzi must have been fascinated by the flourishing musical life of his time, especially opera. A list of musicians included in his large collection, which (according to P. Petrobelli) was to be entitled *Il mondo novo*, includes the composers Jommelli and Pergolesi, the famous castrato Farinelli; Faustina Bordoni, the leading prima donna of the time; stage designer and architect Filippo Juvarra, and players of orchestral instruments. One of the singers is Giacinto Fontana, whose nickname was "Farfallino Perugino"—little butterfly from Perugia. He sang in that same 1723 opera production mentioned in the caption for Vivaldi's portrait.

Eventually Ghezzi willed his large collection of portraits to Pope Benedict XIV, who placed it in the Vatican Library.

True enough, Ghezzi only gave us a sketch, but Pincherle's remark cited at the beginning is to the point. Alert, involved, and energetic, Ghezzi's Vivaldi looks indeed like the person who is said to have composed an opera in five days.

Antonio Vivaldi *by Pier Leone Ghezzi (1723), ink on paper, 11.4 × 7.6 cm on a sheet 27.9 × 20.3 cm, which includes two other sketches, Biblioteca Vaticana, Rome*

Jean-Philippe Rameau

Our portrait of Rameau (1683–1764) for a long time was attributed to Jean Baptiste Chardin; art historians now believe that it was painted by Jacques André Joseph Aved (1702–1766), among the major portraitists of the time and a lifelong friend of Chardin. Aved became a member of the Academy in 1734; on a portrait of 1747 he is referred to as *peintre du roi*. That portrait, of Marc de Villiers, is very similar in style to Aved's Rameau painting. Many famous persons sat for Aved: Louis XV, William IV of Orange, Racine, and the poet J. B. Rousseau.

Eighteenth-century painters, and many earlier artists, portrayed important individuals with the tools of their trade. This was particularly true of musicians, partly, no doubt, because musical instruments have always been considered what we would call photogenic. To show Rameau holding a violin, with the bow and a music manuscript on the table next to him, is quite traditional.

He served as organist, first in his native Dijon where he succeeded his father in 1709, but beginning in 1722, several years before this portrait was painted, he lived in Paris, again serving as organist but also as director of an orchestra. At the time, an orchestra customarily was directed by the leader of the violins, suggested by Rameau's appearance in Aved's portrait.

Though Jean-Philippe Rameau was often referred to as the leading French musician of the late baroque, his reputation for a long time was based largely on his writings on music theory, especially his *Traité de l'harmonie reduite à ses principes naturels* (1722). Only in recent times has his music, especially his dramatic music, received wider appreciation through public performances, including some at the Paris Opéra and other major houses. Today we view Rameau, a contemporary of Bach, as an outstanding composer of music with strong dramatic impact. Late in his life, his operas achieved considerable popularity. André Campra, his elder colleague, predicted: "he will eclipse us all." Rameau was ennobled shortly before his death at the age of eighty-one, an event observed with elaborate memorial services in Paris and other cities. Several eulogies were read and printed.

To judge by contemporary accounts, Rameau was taciturn by nature, a trait also suggested by his appearance in our portrait. He was extremely hesitant to talk about himself, even to his closest family members. As a result, we know very little about the first fifty years of his life. He was tall and very thin: "more like a ghost than a man," as Chabanon put it in his *Elogue* of 1764 (Girdlestone 1980, 561). His appearance has been compared to that of Voltaire and Tartini. There is a drawing, by C. de Tersan, caricature-like, of Voltaire meeting Rameau; it emphasizes his tall, thin figure. Hugues Maret (1766) recalls that "[Rameau's] features were large and marked, announcing his firmness of character; his eyes sparkled with the fire which kindled his soul" (Girdlestone 1957, 509).

Rameau's facial expression seems pensive, quizzical, perhaps calculating, which may represent one facet of his personality.

Other Rameau portraits exist, some of doubtful provenance. One, an oil painting also in Dijon, has been attributed to Greuze, but neither the artist nor the subject have been authenticated. Laurence Libin discusses another portrait, recently rediscovered, which at one time had been ascribed to Nicolas Lancret. The work in question was painted on the inside of a harpsichord lid. The instrument was known to Charles Burney and described by him in 1770: the harpsichord was "painted inside and out with as much delicacy as the finest coach or even snuff-box I ever saw at Paris. . . . On the inside cover . . . is that celebrated composer himself; the portrait is very like, for I saw Rameau in 1764" (Libin, 511). A bust by J. J. Caffieri conveys a more friendly, warmer impression of the composer than our portrait. It may show a somewhat older Rameau.

Jean-Philippe Rameau *by Jacques André Joseph Aved (c. 1725), oil on canvas, 150 × 97 cm, Musée des Beaux-Arts, Dijon*

Johann Sebastian Bach

The portrait reproduced here was painted in 1746, only four years before Johann Sebastian Bach's (1685–1750) death. An inscription on the back of the canvas dates the painting to that year and identifies the artist as E. G. Haussmann. Actually, a fair amount is known about Elias Gottlieb Haussmann (1695–1774). He was a court painter, both in Dresden and in Leipzig, where he did portraits almost exclusively. The majority of Haussmann's numerous portraits are devoted to members of the middle class: prosperous merchants, clergymen, university professors. To carry out these commissions he had a large workshop, which helps explain why Haussmann repeatedly used the same slightly expanded bust-length format for his subjects. As in the *Bach*, all sit well forward, occupying most of the canvas. The same austere color scheme is often repeated from one Haussmann portrait to the next.

In this particular study, there is an undeniable clarity and directness about Haussmann's treatment of the face and eyes of his sitter. Bach's compressed lips, narrow eyelids, and small, focused pupils reveal a certain sternness and strength of character. This may have been as much a product of the portraitist's art as a part of Bach's personality. Certainly the pronounced compositional simplicity which Haussmann bestowed on the *Bach* stands in extreme opposition to the great composer's elaborate polyphonic structures.

Our portrait by Haussmann was painted toward the end of the composer's life when he was at work on his final monumental assays of both canon and fugue. The latter half of Bach's Leipzig period found the composer preoccupied with a growing complexity of counterpoint and a penchant for intellectual arrangement of his thematic material. These features reached their height in one of the greatest tests of mental and manual coordination in the history of music, the *Art of Fugue*, on which Bach worked from roughly the time Haussmann painted his portrait until the composer's death. It was also during this period that he produced his masterful canons, best represented by the *Musical Offering* and the *Goldberg Variations*. Bach holds a late, six-part canon, BWV 1076, in his hand in this portrait.

The occasion for the original Haussmann portrait is not altogether certain. It was painted one year before Bach joined Lorenz Mizler's Society of Musical Sciences and may have been presented to that group as one of the requirements for membership. This might help explain the number of silver buttons, fourteen, found on the jacket. Bach was the Society's fourteenth member; in numerical equivalents the letters of his name also add up to fourteen (with *B* valued at two, *A* at one, *C* at three, and *H* at eight). The "Puzzle Canon" which he holds in his right hand was also presented to Mizler's group.

Many copies of the Haussmann portrait exist, at least two of which were done in Bach's lifetime, either by Haussmann or by members of his workshop. These served as the basis for later eighteenth- and nineteenth-century copies. Many inauthentic portraits, those for which the master did not sit but which he inspired, were done after his death. The earliest engraving of Bach, done in 1774 by S. G. Kütner, seems but an awkward version of the Haussmann, reversed as a consequence of the printmaking technique.

At first it may seem surprising that no great artists painted portraits of a composer as distinguished as Bach, but the reasons for this are numerous. During his lifetime, Bach was better known as a performer than as a composer, having published no more than ten works before his death. Equally important, Bach, a devout Lutheran, was born, lived, and worked exclusively in northern Germany. The tradition of portraiture was not as developed as in the south, particularly in Italy and Spain. An aversion to painted likenesses was partially a product of conservative, almost ascetic attitudes found in northern Germany and reinforced by the teachings of John Calvin and Martin Luther. In reacting against the practices of Catholicism, both Protestant reformers saw little justification for either painting or sculpture in the service of the new religion.

Johann Sebastian Bach by E. G. Haussmann (1746), oil on canvas, 76 × 63 cm, Museum für Geschichte der Stadt Leipzig, Leipzig

George Frideric Handel

After beginning his career in his native Germany, George Frideric Handel (1685–1759) spent several years in Italy, broadening his knowledge and experience. Italian music and musicians then reigned throughout the Western world. A brief period of employment in Hanover, Germany, followed in 1710, but Handel, by then known in musical circles as *il caro Sassone* (the dear Saxon) was not satisfied with staying there. He benefited, however, from contacts with members of the House of Hanover, including the future Kings George I and II of England, and Queen Caroline.

Handel first visited London in 1710–11. The musical life of the large, flourishing city had attracted the young Handel as it was to attract the sixty-year-old Haydn at the end of the century. By this time Handel was a known, successful composer and performer. Mainwaring, his early

(though not always accurate) biographer relates Handel's earlier enthusiastic reception in Rome (1706), but his great rise to fame took place in England where he was to remain for the rest of his life. Mainwaring also tells us that

> HANDEL had an uncommon brilliancy and command of finger: but what distinguished him from all other players who possessed these same qualities, was that amazing fulness, force, and energy, which he joined with them. And this observation may be applied with as much justness to his compositions, as to his playing. (P. 62)

Energy and force are qualities that also speak to us from most Handel portraits. Though his long career had its ups and downs, his remarkable successes, in public and at court, are amply documented by many written accounts, but also by the major Handel portraits and their histories.

Thomas Hudson (1701–1779) is chiefly known as the teacher of Sir Joshua Reynolds (1723-1792) and as an able portraitist. Hudson did several major portraits of Handel. Deutsch quotes from the minutes of the General Committee of the Foundling Hospital (1750) that "Mr. Handel had consented to sit for [Hudson]» (Deutsch, *Handel*, 687). The portrait in question, now in Hamburg, conveys the impression of a strong, commanding personality. On the sheet music below Handel's left hand we read the title: *Messiah, an Oratorio*.

The full-length portrait reproduced here dates from 1756; by then Handel was blind. The pose is formal in the style customary at the time. Handel looks all the more imposing since he is seated at a higher level than the viewer. His dress is elaborate; the left hand rests in his coat opening, à la Napoleon; the right hand holds a cane with a gold handle. A sword is at his left side. He wears the extremely large wig for which he was famous. Once more, a score of *Messiah* is included.

In the last codicil to his will, added a few days before his death, Handel expressed his hope that he would be buried in Westminster Abbey, as indeed he was. His monument there, near Poets' Corner, was executed by Louis François Roubiliac (1695–1762) in 1761; it was the sculptor's last major work. His rendering of Handel's face was considered to be especially lifelike. Roubiliac had also done the Handel statue originally placed in Vauxhall Gardens (1738). His 1739 marble bust of Handel was owned by the composer and was eventually given to King George III.

George Frideric Handel as "The Harmonious Boar." Caricature by Joseph Goupy, 1754

Today Handel's oratorio *Messiah* is his best known work, indeed the most famous of all oratorios. Roubiliac's Handel monument in Westminster Abbey shows the composer holding the music for what probably is the best known aria from that work: "I know that my Redeemer liveth."

In the painting reproduced here, and even more so in Hudson's 1748 portrait, we are aware of Handel's heavy, corpulent appearance. Some contemporary descriptions dwell on this, ascribing it at least in part to the composer's fondness for food and drink. What worried observers during his last weeks and months was his "total loss of appetite, which was come upon him, and which must prove more pernicious to a person always habituated, as he had been, to an uncommon portion of food and nourishment" (Mainwaring, 139–140). As often happens, a famous man's weaknesses are readily pounced upon, resulting, in Handel's case, in a number of caricatures such as Joseph Goupy's "The Harmonious Boar" (a later version is entitled "The Charming Brute"). It shows a pig or boar playing the organ, sitting on a wine cask, surrounded by various objects symbolizing gluttony and vanity.

Portraits of eighteenth-century celebrities, as well as other successful paintings, customarily were also issued and sold as engravings, thereby achieving wider circulation (as photographs were to do later) and providing additional income to the artist. Hudson's paintings of Handel likewise became widely known as engravings. For the same reasons casts were made of famous pieces of sculpture, the Handel busts by Roubiliac serving as examples.

Hudson painted musicians and others associated with Handel, including John Pepusch, another German who resided in England. Pepusch became best known for providing the musical arrangements for *The Beggar's Opera* (1728). Charles Jennens, who provided the text for *Messiah* and other Handel compositions, was portrayed by Hudson in 1747. In fact, Jennens had commissioned the full-length portrait reproduced here. Hudson also left us paintings of singers who appeared in works by Handel. Well known among these is Susannah Cibber, soloist in the first *Messiah* performance in Dublin and in later London performances. John Beard, likewise painted by Hudson, was a tenor who sang in many Handel operas and oratorios from 1734 on.

George Frideric Handel *by Thomas Hudson (1756), oil on canvas, 238.8 × 146.1 cm, National Portrait Gallery, London*

Domenico Scarlatti

Painted in high rococo fashion, this portrait of Domenico Scarlatti (1685–1757) presents the composer standing confidently to the left of a harpsichord. He rests one hand on the instrument, which is apparently of Italian origin. In the other he holds a letter addressed "al Signor D. Domenico Scarlatti." This pose, and the embroidered waistcoat and jewelry, convey both an air of confidence and mild aristocratic pretension. The peripatetic Dr. Charles Burney noted that, in the years before his death, Scarlatti was too fat to cross his hands at the keyboard, a practice often required in his sonatas. Though presumably done fifteen years earlier than this, Domingo Antonio de Velasco's portrait shows a relatively slender subject whose long fingers and gaunt face display little inclination toward obesity.

The fourth son of Alessandro Scarlatti, Domenico was the last important composer in the family of famous Italian baroque musicians. Perhaps more is known about Domenico through his music than through surviving records that document his life. He was born in Naples in 1685 and, between the ages of sixteen and thirty-six, enjoyed the patronage of various courts in Naples, Venice, Florence, and Rome. In 1719 he traveled to Portugal. With the exception of three short visits to Italy, he would remain on the Iberian peninsula for the remainder of his life. Employed by King John V in Lisbon, he was charged with the musical education of the Infanta Maria Barbara. When the Infanta married the Spanish Crown Prince Fernando, Scarlatti moved to Madrid as part of Maria Barbara's retinue.

Surprisingly little is known of Scarlatti's activities, either in Lisbon or in Madrid. While at these two courts, he was apparently content to lead a retiring life, meeting the various demands made on him by his royal patrons. At the same time he raised a family of nine children by two wives, and composed music. Chief among his works of this period was the collection of harpsichord pieces, *Essercizi per gravicembalo* (published in London in 1738). This volume was dedicated to his patrons, now the prince and princess of the Austrias. In his preface, Scarlatti himself revealed the purpose of his *Exercises:* "[through] ingenious jesting with art, to accommodate you to the mastery of the harpsichord" (Kirkpatrick, 102). The thirty sonatas that make up the *Exercises* are uniformly high in quality and inspiration. They represent less than five percent of the total number of keyboard sonatas, 555, that have come down to us. The majority of these were copied out in thirteen volumes of thirty sonatas each between 1752 and 1757, the year of Scarlatti's death. Because we know so little about the dates of most of the sonatas, considerable scholarly controversy has grown up in the last twenty-five years concerning various methods of ordering and dating them.

Two other important events happened in Scarlatti's life in chronological proximity to publication of the *Exercises.* In March 1738, Emperor John V of Spain conferred on Domenico Scarlatti the order of Santiago. Slightly more than a year later, his first wife died (he would marry again in 1742).

Even less is known about the artist of our portrait, Domingo Antonio de Velasco (dates unknown). Because of Scarlatti's appearance here, the painting can be dated sometime soon after he was knighted. According to Professor Rinaldo dos Santos, president of the Fine Arts Academy, Lisbon, Scarlatti would have been allowed to wear the fine clothes shown in the portrait only after he had been elevated to the Order of Santiago.

The portrait was in possession of members of the Scarlatti family until its sale in 1912. When Ralph Kirkpatrick published his monumental study, *Domenico Scarlatti*, in 1953, the painting had disappeared from view. Sometime later it went to the collection of José Relvas, the Portuguese ambassador to Spain, and now resides in the Instituiçao José Relvas, Alpiarça, Portugal.

Domenico Scarlatti *by Domingo Antonio de Velasco (c. 1740), oil, Collection José Relvas, Alpiarça, Portugal*

Jean-Jacques Rousseau

Jean-Jacques Rousseau (1712–1778) is best known for his provocative ideas in the disciplines of philosophy, political science, education, sociology, and literature. Yet he was also a musician and composer whose ideas about musical reform were, in the end, of greater consequence than his compositions. He wrote two (lost) symphonies, a variety of vocal works, and seven operas or variants on that form.

As the preponderance of his compositions for voice and stage indicate, Rousseau's vision of music was essentially vocal. His earliest and perhaps his only semiformal training was given by a local choir master. At times throughout his life, Rousseau made money copying music. He also gave musical instruction in his youth.

The great philosophe had worked at compositions for the musical stage since the age of eighteen. His first moderate success came with *Les fêtes de Ramire,* a revision of Rameau's *La Princesse de Navarre,* on which he actually worked with that great baroque composer. It was Rousseau's own *Le devin du village* (The Village Soothsayer) that established his reputation as a composer, a reputation that would last throughout his life. *Le devin* was first performed in 1752, the year before de La Tour painted Rousseau. The inspiration for *Le devin* came from Pergolesi's *La serva padrona.* In his *Confessions,* Rousseau explains that he was staying with the amateur musician, François Mussard. After discussing Pergolesi's opera, Rousseau was unable to sleep. He went for a late night walk and sketched out three pieces that were to find their way into *Le devin.* On hearing them, Mussard encouraged Rousseau, who recounts:

> I was so animated by the encomiums I received that, in six days, my drama, excepting a few couplets, was written.... All I had further to do to it, after my return to Paris, was to compose a little of the recitative, and to add the middle parts, the whole of which I finished with so much rapidity that in three weeks my work was ready for representation. (Rousseau, 356)

The brief opera represents one of Rousseau's principal philosophic ideas: simplicity. Its story of love lost and love regained has only three characters: a shepherd, a shepherdess, and the title role of the village soothsayer. While there is dance and background singing, these are intentionally reduced to concentrate dramatic attention on the reunited peasant couple.

In part, this simplified conception of opera derives from Rousseau's lack of formal musical training. It also registers his reaction against the artificiality, pomp, and elaboration that characterized the staging of French opera, especially that written for the court at midcentury. A single performance of *Le devin* quickly reveals the reasons it became so popular. In addition to its appealing arias, it emphasizes two other themes that would dominate Rousseau's philosophy: the return to nature and the dignity of simple living.

Maurice-Quentin de La Tour (1704–1788) first treated Rousseau in an equally unassuming manner, without the flamboyance or the concentration on surface textures that characterized the rococo, then at its height. Granted, the portrait was too pretty for Rousseau's fellow philosophe, Diderot. In his *Essay on Painting,* Diderot would comment on a later version of the same painting, also by de La Tour, claiming that the artist "has made his portrait of M. Rousseau a beautiful object.... I saw the composer of *Le devin du village* well dressed, well powdered..." (Diderot, vol. 10, 483). According to Maurice Cranston, Rousseau himself was unhappy with the portrait, thinking it more appropriate that he should be seated on a rock rather than on a fashionable chair.

Despite contemporary opinion, the pastel today shows the human side of the composer-philosopher, so apparent in his *Confessions.* An easy smile graces his handsome lips; his large pupils glint engagingly. More than in any composer's portrait through the mid-eighteenth century, the *Rousseau* virtually eliminates all distance between the sitter and the frame. No room, no chair, no elaborately painted details of clothing are allowed to come between Rousseau and his admiring public. Confident, but not overbearing, Rousseau is perhaps animated by the success of *Le devin.*

Part of this animation stems from de La Tour's technique, drawing with pastels. This was a favorite medium during the rococo, revitalized by Rosalba Carriera who introduced it to French artists. While de La Tour was studying in Paris, he developed and helped popularize the technique among fellow rococo portraitists. Elected a member of the Royal Academy in 1746, de La Tour showed in the Salon from 1737 until 1773. His portrait of Rousseau was presented there in 1753. It may, in fact, have been painted at Passy where de La Tour had a country house near that of François Mussard, whose conversation with Rousseau about *La Serva padrona* served as impetus for the French philosophe's popular, indeed revolutionary, *Le devin du village.*

Jean-Jacques Rousseau *by Maurice-Quentin de La Tour (c. 1753), pastel, 45 × 34 cm, Musée Antoine Lécuyer, Saint-Quentin, France*

43

Christoph Willibald Gluck

Portraits of famous composers often exist in several versions. This is particularly true for eighteenth-century artists. A composer may have sat for an oil painting which then was copied and widely distributed in the form of an engraving or, later, lithograph. Likewise, a bust may originally have been executed in marble; then, from a mould, copies in other media, such as bronze, may have been made. Houdon's terra-cotta bust of Gluck (1714–1787) is a good example of such transformations.

Jean-Antoine Houdon (1741–1828) has been called the greatest, the most original French sculptor of the eighteenth century. His talent earned him admission to the French Academy in Rome before he returned to Paris in 1769. During the next two decades he reached the height of his career; his busts are a "gallery of the greatest personalities of the time. Writers, scientists, politicians, businessmen and noble ladies of the *ancien régime* pass in review; . . . there is extraordinary perception in each portrait" (Martinelli vol. 5, 610). Included in this gallery are many political and intellectual leaders, including Diderot, Rousseau, and Voltaire. Houdon even journeyed to Mount Vernon when he was commissioned to do a statue of George Washington.

Houdon's bust of Gluck was commissioned by several of the composer's admirers in Paris, including professional musicians, amateurs, and members of society. The plaster-of-Paris portrait was shown in the Salon of 1775, next to a bust of Sophie Arnaud, one of Gluck's outstanding actor-singers. The base carries the inscription "Houdon, sculpteur du Roy. 1775."

Gluck's appearance, according to some, was heavy: tall, with broad shoulders and a full, round face. Burney compared his appearance to that of Handel: awe-inspiring. But Houdon shows him to us with an informal, natural expression, without wig or ornate collar but with realistic detail, including the many pockmarks on his face. Such realism, also found in other Houdon busts, was resented at the time. A critic in 1775 admitted that the sculpture was very lifelike, but that Houdon should not have paid "such scrupulous attention to the slightest imperfections of the skin. These, the result of an illness, should have been ignored" (Réau, vol. 1, 375). But Houdon said that a lofty purpose of the art of sculpture was to "preserve with all the realism . . . the image of the men who have contributed to the glory or happiness of their country. This idea constantly occupied me and encouraged me in my painstaking work" (Martinelli, vol. 5, 610).

Though Gluck's operas do not form part of today's standard repertory (works that are performed regularly all over the Western world), he became one of the most celebrated composers of his day, rising from obscure beginnings in a Bohemian village to fame and fortune at the courts of Europe.

After years of traveling and holding brief appointments, composing and conducting Italian operas, Gluck settled in Vienna in 1752. He became famous and controversial, in part because of his emphasis on the importance of drama, rather than elaborate singing, in opera.

Though initially successful in Paris, Gluck's operas were not always accepted there, but those qualities that were given unstinting praise were Gluck's, the foreigner's, careful attention to the French language and to the expression of the text's dramatic qualities. Burney noted that "his operas, by conforming to the genius of the French language . . . were received with acclamation. Gluck's music is so truly dramatic, that the airs and scenes, which have the greatest effect on the stage, are cold, or rude, in a concert" (vol. 2, 972–973).

It was during the years when Gluck's lyric tragedies were presented in Paris that his most important portraits were done. Best known

Engraving of Christoph Willibald Gluck by S. C. Miger, based on the painting by Duplessis

Christoph Willibald Gluck *by Jean-Antoine Houdon (1775), terra cotta, unpainted, 67 cm, Royal College of Music, London*

among the authentic paintings of Gluck is that by the French artist Joseph Sifrède Duplessis (1725–1802), done in oil when the composer was sixty-one years old. (There is a fine portrait by Duplessis of Benjamin Franklin, painted in Paris about the same time.) The Gluck portrait was exhibited in the Salon of 1775. Several studies for and copies of the painting exist. An engraving by S. C. Miger (1736–1820) served to give this portrait wide distribution. Miger treats us to a laudatory inscription underneath the portrait, an apt tribute to the composer:

De l'art d'aller au coeur par des accords touchans,
Nul autre mieux que lui n'a montré la puissance;
Et de tous ses rivaux, c'est le seul dont les chants
Ayent charmé son Pays, l'Italie et la France.

(No one knew better how to reach the heart with touching music. Among many rivals, he was the only one whose songs charmed Italy, his home, and also France.)

Houdon's bust was widely admired; it inspired a number of slightly varying reproductions. His own marble copy dates from 1776 or 1777. In the 1777 catalog of his sculptures he noted: "To be placed in the foyer of the Opéra." There is a bronze reproduction in Weimar, and there are others in plaster-of-Paris and painted terra cotta. A medallion by Auguste de Saint-Aubin, based on Houdon's bust, includes the appropriate legend "Il préféra les Muses aux Sirènes" (He preferred the Muses to the Sirens)—that is, noble art to seductive art.

It is fortunate that these and other copies were made, for the marble bust, after having held a place of honor in the foyer of the Paris Opéra for a long time, was destroyed in an 1873 fire there.

Joseph Haydn

In Hardy's painting, executed in the traditional, formal manner of much portraiture from the late eighteenth century, Haydn looks at the viewer with a calm, somewhat quizzical expression. As a composer, he is suitably shown holding a musical score, perhaps (to judge by the format) one of his symphonies that were so enthusiastically received in London.

The Haydn portrait by the English painter Thomas Hardy (birth and death dates unknown) had been commissioned by the music publisher John Bland in 1791. Bland had visited Eszterháza in 1789, eager to publish some of Haydn's compositions and to sign a contract for three new flute trios. Hardy's painting probably was completed early in 1792.

Our visual impression, based on Hardy's rendition, may be augmented by descriptions of others who knew him at this time: Georg August Griesinger and Albert Christoph Dies, two of his early biographers. According to Dies, Haydn was fairly short and heavy set:

> His facial features were quite regular; his expression was animated, even fiery, yet could also be restrained, kind, and inviting. These features expressed dignity when Haydn was in a serious mood, but could also be light and smiling when he was engaged in conversation. I never heard him laugh loudly. (Ladenburger, 301–302)

He goes on to say that his nose was prominent, his skin dark and disfigured by pockmarks.

Griesinger's description is similar, adding that Haydn's forehead was broad and nicely curved. Both writers stress that he was essentially softspoken, serious, and gentle.

In some ways Joseph Haydn's (1732–1809) career resembles that of George Frideric Handel. Both came from humble beginnings; both earned the respect and admiration of music lovers from all walks of life, and both reaped great successes in England. Haydn's earliest childhood years were spent in a small village in Lower Austria; from there his road led, by way of the Imperial Court Chapel in Vienna, followed by hard years of adolescence, to lifelong service at the court of the Eszterházy princely family.

Given his distinguished career, the impressive number of Haydn portraits comes as no surprise—few, understandably, dating from his formative years. Aside from the Eszterházy family, Haydn's supporters and patrons included the imperial court in Vienna. He accumulated great successes and many honors in France and England, including an honorary doctorate from Oxford. There were memberships in honorary societies at home and abroad, commissions for music from faraway places such as Cádiz in Spain. Above all, Haydn was loved and admired everywhere, especially at home. A famous painting by Balthasar Wigand shows the musicians and large audience at a performance of Haydn's *Creation* shortly before the composer's death. To judge by eyewitness accounts it must have been a moving occasion—a warm, heartfelt tribute to the great man.

Somfai gives a detailed inventory of the many Haydn portraits that exist or existed, including busts of wax, marble, and other materials, commemorative medals and medallions, and the composer's death mask. Of the many representations, around twenty-five are authentic. Some of these document Haydn's two extended journeys to England where he was acclaimed by all, including the royal family. The Prince of Wales became one of his special admirers and benefactors.

From Haydn's copious notebooks and letters, and from other sources, we know how pleased the composer was, not only with his musical successes but also with the resulting attention paid to him. The Prince of Wales had commissioned John Hoppner to paint Haydn's portrait. One day, as he was about to leave for a sitting, Haydn "anxiously looked at himself in the mirror, saying discontentedly: 'today I don't look well; I won't go to see Hoppner'" (Somfai, 220).

After his return to Austria, Haydn was painted by Johann Zitterer, among others. This portrait shows a surprisingly young-looking Haydn—for a good reason, according to his early biographer, Carpani:

> Haydn disliked being pictured as an old man. He returned one painting to the artist who had portrayed him as he really was in the year 1800, i.e., in his seventieth [sic] year. Haydn told him quite calmly that, if an honest man wanted to have his portrait done, one should not choose that time in his life when he looked least attractive—that this bordered on treason. Somewhat excitedly he added: "If I was Haydn by the time I was forty, why do you want to show a seventy-year-old Haydn? Neither you nor I stand to gain from this." The painter had to give in, and now all the world can observe, on the title page of Artaria's edition of Haydn's Opus 75, the comic consequences of these reproaches. (Quoted by Ladenburger, 306)

Still in 1792 Hardy made an engraving based on his oil painting, a widespread custom, as we observed in connection with Handel. Engravings of other Haydn portraits were offered for sale in Vienna, in 1781 and often thereafter, by publishers who carried Haydn compositions in their catalogs. The composer was fond of a

Franz Joseph Haydn *by Thomas Hardy (c. 1791), oil on canvas, 76.5 × 63.5 cm, Royal College of Music, London*

drawing of himself by George Dance; he was eager to have an engraving made of it so that it might be included in an edition of his piano compositions. The Hardy portrait was used as a frontispiece for the first edition of Haydn's *Creation* in 1800.

There are several other Hardy portraits of musicians associated with Haydn who were well regarded in London at the time, including Johann Peter Salomon (1792), the violinist and impresario who had been the moving spirit behind Haydn's journeys to England; Muzio Clementi (1794), who had long been successful in England as a pianist and composer, and William Cramer (1794), violinist-leader of the *Professional Concert*. Hardy exhibited both Haydn's and Salomon's portraits at the Royal Academy.

John Christian Bach

A glance at Gainsborough's portrait suffices to indicate that [John Christian] Bach moved with easy grace in a society to which his profession was ordinarily admitted on another footing. The elegant distinction of his dress, his confident pose, betoken a man accustomed to the drawing-rooms of the "Nobility and Gentry," the patrons of his enterprises.

CHARLES SANFORD TERRY

In the 1740s and '50s, mention of the name Bach was more likely to bring to mind one or the other of Johann Sebastian Bach's sons, especially Carl Philipp Emanuel or Johann (later John) Christian. They were indeed born at the end of an age in which their great father represented a late flourishing of baroque style. If his music was considered old-fashioned and "learned" by many contemporaries, that of the youngest son, John Christian, clearly points to the future, to the age of Mozart.

After his father's death, the fifteen-year-old John Christian Bach (1735–1782), already an aspiring musician, was sent to Berlin to live and study with his brother Emanuel, harpsichordist to King Frederick, "The Great." John's musical education was furthered by the active musical life at the Prussian court, at which the king's taste for Italian music set the style. By 1756 we find John in Milan and Bologna, studying with (Padre) Giovanni Battista Martini whose fame as composer and teacher attracted pupils from many countries. A friendship, based on mutual esteem, developed between the two musicians.

These years in Italy brought successes to the young composer, chiefly as a writer of Italian operas. He also was appointed organist at Milan cathedral. But like Handel before him (and Haydn after him), he was attracted to England, regarded as a country where foreign musicians, Germans and Italians in particular, could find ample opportunities.

He arrived in London in 1762 and soon became music master to Queen Sophie Charlotte, herself a German princess. Italian opera formed an important part of London's musical life; John Christian soon was able to bring out his own works in that genre. He also organized public concerts and composed and published works for the then-new fortepiano. When the boy wonder Mozart appeared in London in 1764 he was befriended by Bach; in time a warm friendship developed. Later their paths were to cross again on the Continent.

During Bach's years in England, Thomas Gainsborough (1727–1788) was establishing himself as a foremost painter of landscapes and portraits. He was an original member of the Royal Academy, founded in 1768. Commissions from the royal family testify to his reputation; he also is said to have given drawing lessons to the queen. Success is also reflected in the steadily rising fees his portraits (of which he did about 800) commanded, fees close to those charged by Sir Joshua Reynolds, his lifelong rival. But such success also had its drawbacks. Gainsborough, who was very fond of music and a capable performer on several instruments, wrote to his musician-friend William Jackson that he had to devote too much time to such commissions, and that he would rather

> take my viol-da-gamba and walk off to some sweet village, where I can paint landskips and enjoy the fag-end of life in quietness and ease. But these fine ladies and their tea drinkings, dancings, husband-huntings etc, will fob me out of the last ten years. . . . But we can say nothing, . . . only, d——it I hate . . . being confined in harness to follow the track whilst others ride in the waggon . . . gazing at green trees and blue skies without half my *Taste*. (Millar, 11)

At times, Bach would listen to Gainsborough's playing, and after interrupting him "with an occasional ironical 'Bravo!' would push the painter from his seat at the harpsichord, to deliver one of his own, more inspired improvisations" (Whitley, 120). Gainsborough's passionate love of music was noted by several of his friends and acquaintances. William Jackson thought that at times it exceeded his devotion to painting.

Gainsborough's portrait of Bach was painted at the request of Padre Martini—a request that surely honored the pupil. It must have come around 1776; apparently the portrait was to be hung at the Liceo Musicale in Bologna.

The portrait pleased the composer greatly. He must have asked Gainsborough to provide a replica, for the portrait, still in Bologna today, is virtually identical with one Bach kept for himself, which is now in the collection of Lord Hillingdon.

In this rather formal portrait Bach seems to listen to, or observe, someone to the viewer's left. The facial expression is firm, somewhat questioning, but not unfriendly. Many of Gainsborough's half portraits, such as this one, are formally posed, while his full-size portraits tend to be more relaxed, especially those he painted of his friends and acquaintances. Aristocratic patrons, one supposes, preferred a more traditional, formal rendering.

Gainsborough portrayed other musicians. His painting of Carl Friedrich Abel is of the more casual kind: Abel, a friend, was the last great player of the viola da gamba, an instrument that

John Christian Bach *by Thomas Gainsborough (c. 1776), oil on canvas, 72 × 62 cm, Civico Museo Bibliografico Musicale, Bologna*

soon was to disappear from general use. In Gainsborough's painting (1777) he is seated, writing music, smiling, with his gamba at his side. Another musician-friend, Johann Christian Fischer, was an oboist of international fame. He, too, is shown with his instrument, friendly and relaxed, leaning on a keyboard instrument by the London maker Joseph Merlin.

Joan Reis recently has called attention to a possible third portrait of Bach by Gainsborough, previously thought to represent David Middleton, surgeon-general to King George III.

49

Luigi Boccherini

In his youth, when this portrait was executed, Luigi Boccherini (1743–1805) was known primarily as a cellist. He probably received his earliest instruction from his father, also a cellist, in the city of his birth, Lucca. He continued his studies in that famous Tuscan city, moving to Rome at age fourteen. Between 1757 and 1763 he worked with his father in the court theater in Vienna. The following year he was appointed as cellist by the Grand Council of the City of Lucca. It was probably during the next three years, while he served the Grand Council, that this portrait was painted.

If that is the case, and the youthful features of the sitter indicate that it is, Boccherini was captured at a turning point in his career. In 1765 he arranged and played in the earliest string quartet performances in Milan. Also while in the employ of Lucca he composed two oratorios and a cantata. The majority of Boccherini's sacred works would be written during his three-year sojourn in Lucca. Later, his interests would turn almost exclusively to chamber music.

Chamber music naturally was written to be performed *in camera*, in the drawing rooms of aristocracy, who commissioned, arranged, or paid for such performances. Boccherini is painted as if performing at such an occasion. Here he wears clothing fashionable in aristocratic society at the height of the rococo: a flaring coat, an embroidered waistcoat, an elaborate cravat, breeches.

In its posed artificiality, the setting, while understated, is typical of the period. Boccherini is not seated in a lavishly appointed salon; rather he poses on a half-enclosed porch which hints at a landscape behind the performer. Only the apparel and setting of this portrait are rococo. Its clarity of focus and directness contain hints of neoclassicism, just then starting to take hold in Italy.

It was in Rome in particular that much of the theory of eighteenth-century classicism developed. Pompeo Batoni (1708–1787), who may have been responsible for the *Boccherini,* was a leader of this new tradition. In Rome as early as 1728, Batoni developed a classical style that influenced Anton Raffael Mengs, Gavin Hamilton, and the author of the important *Thoughts on the Imitation of Greek Works* (1755), Johann Winckelmann.

Batoni also came from Boccherini's native town, Lucca. He moved to Rome where he set up a fashionable workshop on Via Bocca de Leone in 1760. He could have visited Lucca sometime in the mid-1760s and painted Boccherini's portrait as cellist of the Grand Council. Less likely, Boccherini could have returned to Rome where he had studied for two years as a teenager. Artists as diverse as the Longhis and Sebastiano Ceccarini have also been suggested as the authors of this portrait.

At first glance, Boccherini appears to be holding his cello in the usual position. Closer inspection, however, will reveal that the instrument is pinioned between the performer's calves, its back resting on his left thigh. The end pin, on which the cello sits in contemporary performance, was not invented until the nineteenth century.

Luigi Boccherini, *Italian (c.1764–67), oil on canvas, 133.3 × 90.7 cm, National Gallery of Victoria, Melbourne*

Giovanni Paisiello

In her *Memoirs,* Louise-Elisabeth Vigée-Lebrun (1755–1842) relates that she began her portrait of the composer Giovanni Paisiello (1740–1816) in December 1790. He sat in her recently rented apartment, which was so cold both model and painter had to warm their hands by blowing on them and finally by starting a fire. One glance at the portrait reveals Vigée-Lebrun's true gift. Paisiello sits at a clavichord. In typical late-eighteenth-century fashion, he looks, not at the music or the keyboard, but to his left and up. This pose is intended to show him communicating with some unseen object outside the painting, a standard device in portraits of artists to reveal them in moments of inspiration. His mouth is open; his eyes are transfixed. Placed with apparent nonchalance, several of his compositions rest on top of the clavichord. One is open to its title page, revealing it to be the score to the opera *Nina, o sia La pazza per amore.* The other is the *Te Deum,* on which Paisiello was at work when Vigée-Lebrun painted him. There is about the feigned casual nature of the portrait an ultimately late-rococo air of artificiality appropriate to Vigée-Lebrun's connections with the aristocracy and the royal family of France.

Vigée-Lebrun was among the most colorful artists to live in France at the end of the eighteenth and beginning of the nineteenth centuries. She was a court portraitist and most favored painter of Queen Marie Antoinette in the decade before the French Revolution. During the 1780s the artist owned two elegant townhouses, in which she hosted a popular Parisian salon that included eminent actors, musicians, and writers. She fled France in the face of the Revolution to become a celebrated emigré wherever she went: Austria, England, Germany, Italy, Russia, Switzerland.

Because of her court position, her royalist sympathies, and her revulsion at the bloody events of the Revolution, Vigée-Lebrun traveled to Italy in 1789. She settled in Rome but frequently visited the southern part of the peninsula. On her second trip to Naples, she painted the famous composer of opera and religious music, Giovanni Paisiello, who held the joint positions of Composer of Music Drama and Master of the Royal Chapel at the court of Ferdinando IV. Before Vigée-Lebrun painted his portrait, Paisiello, a prolific composer of opera, had enjoyed wide success with *La serva padrona,* (the other) *Il barbiere de Seviglia,* and *Il re Teodoro.* The artist met Paisiello immediately after she had attended his opera, *Nina, o sia La pazza per amore,* which explains the reason its title page is displayed so prominently on the clavichord. This particular opera, his seventy-third, was written when the composer was a mere forty-eight.

Vigée-Lebrun was eminently qualified to paint the prolific Neapolitan composer. She frequently did portraits of artists of different callings. In 1785, she even painted André Ernest Modeste Grétry, the leading composer of *opéra comique.* A much more modest undertaking than the *Paisiello,* the portrait of Grétry shows Vigée-Lebrun capable of intimate studies of warmth, charm, and understated humor. She also portrayed the great soprano Angelica Catalani, and the painters Hubert Robert and Joseph Vernet.

The *Giovanni Paisiello* was displayed in the Salon, the principal government-sponsored annual exhibition in Paris, in 1791, the year it was completed. There it achieved recognition as one of the most acclaimed portraits of that particular Salon. In relating the *Paisiello* to the work of a Dutch master of the baroque, the tract, *La Béquille de Voltaire au Salon,* proclaimed of Mme. Vigée-Lebrun: "O Van Dyck, you are born again" (Baillio, 95).

Giovanni Paisiello *by Louise-Elisabeth Vigée-Lebrun (1791), oil on canvas, 130 × 100 cm, Musée National des Châteaux de Versailles*

Domenico Cimarosa

To realize the "high ideal" of antiquity, strength is imperative; and Cimarosa had discovered it in the themes of his opera Gli Orazi e Curiazi. . . . *Canova found the courage to abandon the "high ideal" of antique sculpture.*

STENDHAL, 1824

Antonio Canova (1757–1822) was venerated in his time, perhaps the most successful sculptor of his age. He continued to be held in high esteem during the heyday of romanticism, but then fell out of favor. Admiration of his work led to numerous prestigious commissions, such as the monument to Pope Clement XIII in St. Peter's in Rome (1792). He left the Eternal City at the time of the French invasion but managed to avoid Cimarosa's troubles mentioned below. More than that, he was summoned to Paris to do a bust of Napoleon. Commissions for statues, busts, and monuments came from many countries. In 1820 Canova created a marble monument of George Washington, later destroyed by fire.

Canova's small marble bust of Cimarosa is striking because of its realism, unlike many of his better-known neoclassic works which come closer to Stendhal's ideal of antiquity. There is no attempt to hide the composer's corpulent, rather unattractive appearance; there is no sentimentality. The face seems almost expressionless, surprising for the composer of so much lively, vivacious music. It is quite different from the same artist's bust of Pope Pius VII, done a few years earlier, characterized by lively facial expression, carefully detailed and revealing something about the pontiff's character.

In Domenico Cimarosa (1749–1801) we once more have a composer whose reputation was international during his lifetime but whose music gradually disappeared from the repertory. Today the overture to *Il matrimonio segreto* (The Secret Marriage), popular with symphony orchestras, is the chief reminder of his fame.

Cimarosa was born in Naples; his first opera was performed there in 1772. His successes led to an invitation in 1787 to go to St. Petersburg as maestro di cappella at the court of Catherine II. Four years later he left Russia for Vienna, to serve the Austrian emperor Leopold II. In December 1791, a correspondent for a Berlin weekly reported from Vienna that Cimarosa, the new Kapellmeister, was expected to arrive any day: "German musicians and composers are likely to be in for hard times" (Deutsch, *Dokumente*, 358). Leopold was no great lover of opera, but he preferred Cimarosa to Salieri, who had to give up the direction of the court opera. *The Secret Marriage*, first given in 1793, became Cimarosa's most popular opera; at one time it was performed on 110 successive evenings—a feat unheard-of in the days before long-run Broadway musicals.

Cimarosa returned to Italy in 1793 (probably much to Salieri's relief), at a time of great political upheavals there, such as those that form the background of Puccini's opera *Tosca*. He became involved in politics, narrowly escaped execution but was imprisoned for four months in 1799.

Haydn gave many Cimarosa operas at Eszterháza. Goethe was fond of them; he translated and staged one of them in Weimar.

According to Elena Bassi, the Cimarosa bust was the first in a series depicting famous men, created for Rome's Pantheon. It was placed there, some fifteen years after the composer's death, between the busts of two other opera composers famous at the time: Sacchini and Paisiello.

Stendhal, an admirer of both the composer and the sculptor but not always a reliable chronicler, recalled (in his *A Roman Journal*, 1829) that the bust was created at the instigation of Cardinal Consalvi, who later became instrumental in saving Cimarosa from the death sentence. Consalvi, very fond of music,

> used to go quite often in the evening to the home of Madame . . . , the ambassador's wife; there he would meet a charming young man who knew by heart some twenty of the immortal Cimarosa's finest arias; Rossini—for he it was—would sing those that the cardinal requested, while His Excellency would settle himself comfortably in a big armchair, somewhat in the shade. After Rossini had sung for a few minutes, one would see a silent tear escape from the minister's eyes and flow slowly down his cheek. (*Roman Journal*, 307)

Among artists who painted portraits of Cimarosa, Alessandro Longhi is the best known; the work, formerly in the Liechtenstein museum, was sold in 1945 and cannot be located at present. There is another portrait by the well-known artist Elisabeth Vigée-Lebrun, just considered, done for the French Academy.

Domenico Cimarosa by Antonio Canova (1808), marble, 59 cm, Protomoteca Capitolina, Rome

Antonio Salieri

The serious, melancholic expression on Salieri's face suggests weariness, perhaps disappointment, yet the event in 1816 that was the occasion for the portrait was entirely joyful: Salieri's fiftieth anniversary of service in the Habsburg court.

> He was one of the most important opera composers of the late 18th century. His works were performed throughout Europe—from Naples to Copenhagen, from Lisbon to Moscow. He was feted in Paris as the distinguished successor to Gluck. For years his works were phenomenal box office successes at the Paris Opéra, before, during and after the French Revolution. . . . But the center of his activities was Vienna . . . where he was in charge of Italian opera, became Court Kapellmeister, even was among the founders of the Gesellschaft der Musikfreunde. For decades he was the most influential personality in the imperial city's musical life—much in demand as a teacher. Among his pupils were Beethoven, Hummel, Moscheles and Schubert; even the young Liszt received instruction from him. (Braunbehrens, 18)

It is curious, and perhaps unique in the annals of music, that a composer thus celebrated, who then fell into fairly general oblivion, should recapture the interest and imagination of a worldwide public for two reasons: the persistent rumor, going back to his time, that he had poisoned his "arch rival" Mozart—and the phenomenal success of the film *Amadeus* which, while making no claim to historical accuracy, presents fascinating if controversial portraits of the two composers. Nearly a century earlier, the story of Mozart's poisoning had even inspired Rimsky-Korsakov to compose an opera, *Mozart and Salieri* (1898).

Salieri wrote his own first opera in 1769, for performance at court. In time his successful career led him to the top position there. His voice students were legion, but he also taught piano, theory, and composition. Beethoven was anxious to benefit from Salieri's knowledge and practical experience, especially regarding vocal composition. He studied with him for many years, off and on, at least until 1802, and dedicated his violin sonatas Op. 12 to him.

In 1816, Salieri's Habsburg anniversary was observed with great splendor. Schubert, also one of his students, described the event in his diary and composed a cantata for the occasion. Mähler's Salieri portrait must have been painted in or after 1816, because the composer is shown wearing the golden chain and medal of honor bestowed on him on the occasion of the fifty-year jubilee. He is similarly depicted in a painting by Natale Schiavoni, reproduced in Braunbehrens' biography.

After an extended illness Salieri died on May 7, 1825. By then his operas were going out of favor with the Viennese public, while Mozart's operatic star had begun to rise steadily after his early death in 1791. To the aging Salieri this must have been hard to swallow.

It is an indication of Salieri's stature that a long, laudatory obituary appeared in the Vienna *Allgemeine Theaterzeitung* soon after his death. Angermüller quotes it in its entirety.

Willibord Joseph Mähler (1778–1860) is best known for his several portraits of Beethoven to whom he was introduced in 1803. Though an official in the Austrian State Chancellery, he was a talented artist who had studied painting in Dresden and at the Vienna Academy. In August 1815 a writer for the *Allgemeine Musikzeitung* praised Mähler highly, making special mention of his series of portraits of Viennese composers, portraits "distinguished by being eloquent, true to life" (Frimml, 59). Many of these were painted at the behest of Joseph von Sonnleitner, one of the founders of the Gesellschaft der Musikfreunde (Society of the Friends of Music) and best known for his revision of the text for Beethoven's *Fidelio*. Salieri also had been associated with the Gesellschaft since its inception. His portrait today is displayed in the conference room of that institution. Though unsigned it has been established to be by Mähler.

Antonio Salieri by Willibord Joseph Mähler (c. 1816), oil on canvas, 55.5 × 44 cm, Gesellschaft der Musikfreunde, Vienna

Wolfgang Amadeus Mozart

Mozart's career—perhaps the most remarkable of any musician in the Western world—began early and was very short. He died at the age of thirty-five, an age at which few men would have risen to sufficient fame to warrant being immortalized through portraits. But long before the mature portrait shown here, in fact as soon as the incredible musical talents of the small child were noticed, came the first of many portraits. Others followed as word of his talent spread, soon beyond his native Salzburg and throughout Europe. The boy Mozart was portrayed twice in 1763; one a very formal oil painting, in Salzburg, the other, a watercolor done in Paris, with father Leopold and sister "Nannerl."

These and other youth portraits are charming, touching. Their lack of realism reflects the custom of the time of representing children (especially young princes and princesses) as small adults. They do not wear children's clothes, and often their appearance and facial expressions are strangely serious. Contemporaries were similarly affected: the great German writer Goethe reminisced about having seen "the little man" Mozart when he was seven years old (Deutsch, *Dokumente*, 470).

Mozart scholars now hold that there are or were twelve authentic (that is, painted-from-life) portraits of the composer. Of these, the one that is generally considered the most lifelike, painted by his brother-in-law Joseph Lange in 1782–83, is unfinished. Lange intended to show Mozart at the keyboard, as several other portraits do, but he completed only the head.

The oil painting reproduced here is unusual in that it was painted after Mozart's death and thus is not authentic in one meaning of the term. Barbara Krafft (1764–1825), though not an internationally famous painter, was highly thought of by Austrian contemporaries. The opinion that hers is the best Mozart portrait goes back to her time. In 1961 Otto Erich Deutsch considered it "the only important posthumous portrait" (*Mozart und seine Welt*, xvi). It is the result of a commission by Josef von Sonnleitner, a Viennese government official, writer, and amateur, active in the city's musical life. Wishing to include a painting of Mozart in his gallery of portraits of famous musicians (a gallery that also included our portrait of Salieri, just discussed), Sonnleitner approached Krafft who then lived in Salzburg. He also turned to Mozart's sister Nannerl for help. From Nannerl's reply to Sonnleitner we know how seriously Krafft took her commission. Nannerl owned three portraits of her brother, done from life, and good likenesses; she put these at Krafft's disposal. The artist studied them carefully. Her goal was to come up with a composite that would do justice to the composer in every way.

By all accounts, Krafft succeeded admirably in providing a complete, realistic portrait. After the composer's death, as his fame increased, many artists felt called upon to provide paintings, engravings, statues, and medallions of the great man. Deutsch counted some forty Mozart portraits that are not authentic, concluding that "had Mozart posed for all of them, Köchel's catalog of his works would have been considerably shorter" (*Mozart und seine Welt*, xi–xii). Many of these later portraits are overly sentimental in a nineteenth-century, romantic way. As we can see, Krafft did not succumb to that temptation. Mozart looks at us quizzically; his appearance is plain—the large nose, mentioned in contemporary descriptions, is accentuated. His erect posture goes with what we know of him—that he was short and had much self-confidence. Deutsch adds that while Mozart's parents had been considered "the handsomest couple in Salzburg" (Nannerl), Wolfgang was "short, slender, with an unhealthy complexion, quite unassuming as to facial features and physique." An embroidered red coat then was the customary attire for a *maestro di musica*; we already see it in the Verona portrait of 1770 and in the family picture of 1780–81.

Sonnleitner played an active part in the founding of Vienna's Society of the Friends of Music. The Krafft portrait today is among its most treasured possessions.

Wolfgang Amadeus Mozart by Barbara Krafft (1819), oil on canvas, 54 × 42 cm, Gesellschaft der Musikfreunde, Vienna

Luigi Cherubini

The tired but indomitable old man; the face, with its sunken cheeks, veiled eyes, and set, down-turned mouth, still bears the traces of the poetic sensibility which distinguished the composer in his youth.
BASIL DEANE

Jean-Auguste-Dominique Ingres (1780–1867) completed this famous portrait of Luigi Cherubini in the year of the composer's death, 1842. The ethereal woman, entering as though from another world, is the Muse of Lyric Poetry, and her dramatic presence in this painting helps to place it clearly in the neoclassic tradition. Subjects taken from antiquity, including Greek and Roman mythology and religion, were favored by artists of this school.

Although Ingres lived during romanticism's great flourishing, he is an outstanding representative of classic (or neoclassic) style in painting. He was a painstaking, meticulous artist and craftsman, ever critical of his own work, ever striving for perfection, as demonstrated by his countless preliminary studies and sketches, for this portrait and others, and by many revisions of completed canvases.

Clarity of line and form, along with elegance and great realism, distinguish his art, revealed here by great attention to details of facial features and of the folds in the Muse's attire. Cherubini appears serious and thoughtful, perhaps skeptical or disappointed; a realistic portrayal according to what we know of the composer and his life. The symbolism of the Muse behind him is in keeping with classic tradition. Her instrument is the lyre, an instrument of antiquity; her extended hand, as in a blessing, symbolizes inspiration—the "kiss of the Muse," to use a phrase still familiar today.

In many ways Ingres continued the principles of neoclassicism established by David in whose atelier he had received his schooling at the age of sixteen. Ingres first established himself as a painter of historical subjects—the highest category, according to the standards of the official French Academy. The composer's success led to many honors: he became a Grand Officer in the Legion of Honor and a member of the Institut de France.

The portrait of Cherubini (1760–1842) testifies to Ingres's great fondness for music and to his admiration for the Italian, to whom he referred as "our great master and, to my glory, my illustrious friend" (Schlenoff, 306). Ingres also expressed himself frequently and enthusiastically about his other favorites—the great classic composers Gluck, Haydn, Mozart, and Beethoven. (Here we might remember that Beethoven was a contemporary, a "modern" composer.) Berlioz, in a letter to Liszt (1839), asked him to "forgive [Ingres] for loathing me when you remember that he adores Gluck and Beethoven." Ingres was an enthusiastic violinist; the French expression "un violon d'Ingres" still today refers to an avocation that is a passion. Ingres's violin is among the important objects, along with his paintings and drawings, exhibited in the Ingres Museum in Montauban, his native city. The painter often hosted musical soirees at home, with Madame Ingres playing the piano. He attended opera performances and concerts but did not like virtuosity for its own sake, and is said to have detested Paganini. Yet Ingres's portrait of him, done in 1819, is among the best likenesses of the great violin virtuoso (see p. 69).

Cherubini was born in Florence at a time when opera was Italy's most important musical genre. He wrote his first opera before he had reached the age of twenty. Seven years before that he had written a solemn Mass. Sacred music continued to be an important part of his oeuvre.

Cherubini settled in Paris in 1787 and soon became swept up in the storms of the revolutionary period. He wrote much music of the kind the new leaders demanded: hymns, marches, and other patriotic works. He became quite successful in official Paris but was unable to gain the favor of Napoleon who was partial to the music of other Italians: Paisiello, Paër, Spontini. Napoleon's continued disapproval, indeed, enmity, was the great disappointment of Cherubini's life; one is tempted to see it reflected in his appearance in our portrait. Nevertheless, Cherubini weathered several changes of regimes and eventually gained a position of distinction as director of the Conservatory which had been established at the time of the Revolution. In Vienna he met Haydn, Mozart, and Beethoven. The latter was outspoken in his admiration for the Italian, declaring him to be "the greatest living composer." Cherubini's *Requiem Mass in C Minor* was performed in Vienna soon after Beethoven's death.

Cherubini and the Muse of Lyric Poetry actually is the second version of this portrait. A year earlier Ingres had completed a painting of the composer in an identical pose, but without the Muse behind him. Today this version is in the Cincinnati Art Museum. Only Cherubini's head was painted by Ingres, the body and hands, "painted after those of Charles Gounod," (see pp. 92f.) having been done by one of his students (Wildenstein, 212). The background of this earlier painting shows scores of several of the composer's most successful operas, including *Les deux journées* and *Médée*.

Luigi Cherubini and the Muse of Lyric Poetry *by Jean-Auguste-Dominique Ingres (completed in 1842), oil on canvas, 105 × 94 cm, Musée du Louvre, Paris*

According to Deane, Cherubini had sat for the second portrait but did not realize that Ingres had added the figure of the muse.

> Thinking to surprise and please his friend, Ingres invited him to view the completed portrait in his studio. Cherubini came, looked at it in silence, turned on his heel and walked out. It was not for Ingres to decide where and when the accolade of the muses should be awarded, he told his family, and retired in a fury to his study. Meanwhile the dismayed painter had dispatched a note of apology to Mme Cherubini.... Some time later Cherubini emerged with a sheet of manuscript. (p. 51)

The music manuscript was a canon in three voices, beginning with the words *"O Ingres amabile, pittor chiarissimo,"* (lovable Ingres, most famous painter), and bearing a dedication to "Dear Ingres, from his grateful admirer, Luigi Cherubini." It was to be Cherubini's last composition.

Earlier portrait of Luigi Cherubini, by J. A. D. Ingres (1841), oil on canvas, 82 × 71.1 cm, Cincinnati Art Museum

Ludwig van Beethoven

Ferdinand Schimon (1797–1852) was not yet twenty-three when he painted this portrait of Beethoven. Then an aspiring artist, the young man also possessed such a fine tenor voice that no one less than Franz Schubert persuaded him to give up painting and instead pursue a career as a singer. We are fortunate enough to know many of the circumstances surrounding the painting of this thoroughly romantic portrait, thanks to Beethoven's amanuensis and first major biographer, Anton Felix Schindler.

According to Schindler's account, it was he who persuaded his master to let himself be painted by Schimon. The artist then followed Beethoven on country walks and also made sketches before he was permitted to set up his easel beside the master's study. Beethoven was then at work on his *Missa Solemnis* and refused to sit for the artist in the conventional way. Working in this disadvantaged manner, Schimon had managed to finish all but Beethoven's eyes when the composer took an interest in the young artist and invited him to have coffee. After two such impromptu breaks, during which Schimon had the opportunity to study his subject, he finally succeeded in capturing the composer's eyes.

By most standards, Ludwig van Beethoven (1770–1827) was not a handsome man. He was squat, his nose was large, and his features were ravaged with pockmarks. Schimon's portrait is, mildly stated, complimentary. The facial scarring has been eliminated, the nose narrowed. While today the portrait may seem highly fanciful, Schindler, who claimed to be Beethoven's constant companion at the time, found that "No other likeness succeeded so well in portraying the characteristic expression of the eyes, the majestic brow, that domicile of so many powerful and hefty ideas, his coloring, the firmly closed mouth and muscular chin" (Schindler, 452). This may well be a bit self-serving on Schindler's part, since he owned Schimon's *Beethoven* at the time his account was written.

At a minimum, Schindler felt the most important features in the portrait were accurate. More generally speaking, however, Schimon was inspired by the ideals of romanticism when he painted this bust. Beethoven's shoulders and head are silhouetted against an imaginary range of misty, snow-capped mountains. Clouds billow implausibly around his head. His tousled, graying hair flutters in the wind. Finally his eyes roll heavenward under their lids. One wonders if this latter effect may not have been a result of the coffee they drank on those two breaks.

Schindler records there were sixty beans to the cup, strong by any standards.

In quintessential romantic fashion, Beethoven has been represented here in a moment of creative transport, communicating with some larger power. Schimon clearly wanted the viewer to believe this force was at least in part responsible for the transcendental qualities which so many have found in that composer's music. Despite its exaggerations, Schimon's visionary image of Beethoven is a truly romantic interpretation of a founder of that same tradition in music.

In fact, the portrait may have been done slightly earlier than the traditional date assigned to it, 1818–1819. Clearly, the Schimon portrait presents a younger-looking, vigorous Beethoven. Two other portraits from the same time are only slightly more naturalistic. In 1818, August von Klöber drew Beethoven for a portrait that has since disappeared. His sketch, however, remains. In it, the composer has the same long wild hair and intense eyes. Later, in 1820, the composer granted another artist, Joseph Stieler, some six sittings for his famous portrait in which Beethoven is shown holding his *Missa Solemnis*. In this painting, the composer seems to have aged beyond the images of him done by von Klöber and Schimon. His hair is much grayer, his face thinner.

All three artists caught Beethoven at a point of resurgence in his creative life. Preoccupied by his growing deafness and court battles over guardianship of his nephew, Karl, Beethoven composed few large-scale works between 1813 and 1818. The only major compositions that fall in this period are the Piano Sonata in A, Op. 101, and the song cycle *An die ferne Geliebte*, both from 1816. In 1818, however, he undertook and completed the monumental Hammerklavier Sonata, Op. 106, and started the *Missa*. Beethoven's change to a more demanding, unclassical type of composition is clearly reflected in the heroic qualities seen in all three of these portraits from the late 1810s.

In her *Changing Image of Beethoven*, Alessandra Comini has shown that these three portraits inaugurated a tradition that gathered momentum throughout the nineteenth century—the representation of Beethoven as a creative genius. Artistic liberties enhanced this cult of genius. Beethoven's hair became more flamboyantly tousled, his eyes more demonic, his features more deeply set and determined as the century progressed.

Ludwig van Beethoven by Ferdinand Schimon (1818–1819), oil on canvas, Beethoven-Haus, Bonn

The culmination of this tradition can be found in Max Klinger's *Beethoven Monument*, which was not completed until seventy-five years after Beethoven's death. In this sense, it is an imaginary portrait. Yet in its visual grandiloquence, it represents the extent to which the mythic cult of Beethoven had grown by the beginning of the twentieth century.

Max Klinger (1857–1920), the German sculptor, painter, and graphic artist, was influenced by various traditions—classicism, realism, symbolism, art nouveau—at different periods in his career. Extremely musical, Klinger played the piano well. He was an admirer of Brahms, and, in 1894, sent him a series of forty-one etchings, entitled *A Brahms Phantasy*, on the subject of his imagined response to Brahms' *Schicksalslied*. In return, Brahms dedicated his *Four Serious Songs* to the artist.

Klinger was also devoted to Beethoven's music. As a young man, he had been introduced to it by his father and often played it on the piano. According to the artist himself, he was at the piano one evening when the idea for his great *Beethoven Monument* came to him, almost in final form.

For the next seventeen years, he worked on the project, making first a plaster model, then traveling to Greece, the Pyrenees, and the Tyrol for the marble. Finally, it was in Paris at the end of 1901 that he had the elaborate throne cast in bronze. These extensive preparations were necessitated both by the grandiose ideas behind the *Monument* and by the lavish materials that went into it.

In true art nouveau fashion, the piece possesses a richly polychromed appearance. Beethoven's head, torso, and feet are carved in white marble from Syros; the composer's feet rest on flecked purple marble; the eagle in front of Beethoven is sculpted from dark marble; finally, his drape is made of striped golden onyx. The throne, with three reliefs decorating the sides and back, is cast in bronze, portions of which are gilded. Finally the angels' heads on the frieze that runs across the top portion of the back of the throne are carved in ivory.

While Klinger's extensive use of decorative materials derived from art nouveau, the scheme of his elaborate iconographic program came from symbolist sources. The back and the two side panels of the throne (not visible in this reproduction) present a seemingly incongruous blend of Christian and classical themes. The left side of the throne illustrates two episodes from the myth of Tantalus, symbolizing hunger and thirst. On the right, the temptation scene from the story of Adam and Eve was, for Klinger, a visual correlate of love and sexual

longing. The throne's rear panel merges the Christian and antique worlds in a representation that combines the crucifixion, (with additional Biblical figures) and a figure of Venus. Here, in late Wagnerian fashion, Klinger fuses themes of love (in the Venus) and death and renunciation (in the crucifixion) to produce his own unique visual *Liebestod* (Comini, *Beethoven*, 397–404).

The seminude Beethoven sits on his throne in otherworldly, almost demoniac transport. The pose has clear parallels in earlier Beethoven portraits, and in the work of Rodin and Michelangelo. Ultimately, however, it refers to the great seated Zeus which Phidias created for the Temple of Zeus at Olympia in the fifth century B.C. An eagle, the attribute of Zeus, sits in front of the Olympian Beethoven, while the angels on the frieze behind would seem to welcome the immortal composer into heaven.

Klinger's *Beethoven Monument* first went on public display in 1902 as the centerpiece of the Vienna Secession's fourteenth exhibition. The Secession was founded by a group of younger artists and architects in 1897. Klinger, who was a member of the group, and his fellow artists rebelled against the more academic styles practiced by many leading Viennese artists of the day. Instead, members of the new Secession movement favored a more open approach that recognized a diversity of styles of art.

On the occasion of the Klinger exhibition, the whole of the new Secession building was turned over to a celebration of the cult of Beethoven. The famous Gustav Klimt painted three walls of the entrance room on a theme loosely derived from the Finale of Beethoven's Ninth Symphony. In his provocative, problematic murals, Klimt depicted a highly symbolic progress of the human race from its "Longing for Happiness" to "Joy." For the same occasion, the composer Gustav Mahler (see pp. 114f.) conducted his own transcription of the Finale to the Ninth, in which wind instruments replaced the human voice. Like Klinger's *Monument* itself, the entire exhibition was conceived in Wagnerian terms as a synthesis of the arts.

Set off by ample space, the *Beethoven Monument* sat in the Secession building's central hall. To front and rear, walls were decorated with mosaic panels created especially for the occasion. One of these, *Sinking Night*, was done by the great operatic set designer, Alfred Roller. As Alessandra Comini pointed out in 1987, the Secession building was transformed into a temple for Klinger's *Monument*, which stood as the early twentieth-century denouement to the mounting nineteenth-century drama that grew up around the figure of Beethoven.

Beethoven Monument
by Max Klinger (1902),
bronze, marble, ivory,
onyx, gold, precious
stones, 310 cm, Museum
der bildenden Künste,
Leipzig

Niccolò Paganini

This awkward, Mephistophelean figure, which resembles a lanky black puppet. . . .

Schubert's friend Eduard von Bauernfeld, who attended Paganini's 1828 concerts in Vienna, thus described his impression of the legendary violinist, going on to say that his bows, at the concert's end, had "a slightly comical effect" (De Courcy, vol. 1, 266). The Delacroix portrait reproduced here, and many others, also suggest awkwardness. This may surprise us, given the incredible command Paganini had of his instrument. But aside from showing awkwardness, the painter's intent clearly was to capture a mood—the dark, almost supernatural mood Paganini's appearance invariably conveyed to his audiences—rather than to provide a careful, formal, detailed portrait.

Niccolò Paganini of Genoa (1782–1840) exemplifies instrumental virtuosity better than anyone before his day and, probably, since then. His appearance on the musical scene, in his native Italy and then through much of Europe, coincided with the development of public concert life as we think of it today: well-known soloists (though not yet star conductors) touring extensively, performing for audiences consisting of anyone willing and able to pay the price of admission. To fill the house, the artist and/or the local manager or sponsor needed to establish an image that would appeal to many, an early form of publicity.

For Paganini, publicity included a generous amount of the sensational: facts, but especially rumors and gossip, about his private life as well as about his musical accomplishments. This was an age when preposterous, superstitious statements might hold more credence than they would today—claims, for instance, that the violinist had made a pact with the devil, thus acquiring superhuman abilities to perform feats of virtuosity never heard before.

Stories of this kind about Paganini are legion. Though they are entertaining (and though some come closer to the truth than the one cited), they tend to overshadow the genuine artistry of the man, vouched for by many eye (and ear) witnesses of unquestioned integrity, including some of the greatest composers of the day who attended concerts Paganini gave in Austria, Germany, France, and England. Schubert, who heard him in Vienna in 1828, was impressed by the violinistic fireworks but commented especially on his expressive playing of the Adagio from one of Paganini's own concertos: "I heard

an angel sing" (Deutsch, *Schubert*, 773).

Paganini's concerts in Paris in 1831 created unheard-of excitement. They were attended by many of the city's leading artists, including painters and musicians whom we encounter elsewhere in this book. Rossini had had a hand in arranging these concerts; as elsewhere they were gala events with doubled admission prices. Paris society attended *en masse;* also in the audience were the composers Liszt, Donizetti, and Auber; the German poet Heine, and the painter Delacroix. George Sand, who then wrote for the newspaper *Figaro*, contributed a series of articles on the incredible virtuoso. De Courcy, in her monumental Paganini biography, quotes (vol. 2, 14–15) from a number of other eyewitness accounts:

> I never saw or heard anything to equal it in all my life. The people have all gone crazy and will make everyone else crazy. . . . He was welcomed with thunderous applause . . . but you should have seen how awkward he was! . . . Someone ought to have painted him. He played divinely (Ludwig Boerne).

> Sell all you possess; pawn everything, but go to hear him! [On violinists who had reached fame before:] They are done for; after Paganini they can no longer be heard (Henri Castil-Blaze).

Eugène Delacroix (1798–1863) was greatly impressed by Paganini's virtuosity, and by the hard work required, even by Paganini, to reach this level. "For an hour every day, nothing but scales," Delacroix noted. Painters, he believed, could learn from this; they also have to "practice" to develop technique.

Delacroix's masterful portrait of the violinist resulted from this experience. It is usually dated 1832; Johnson believes it may actually have been done immediately after the painter attended Paganini's first Paris concert in 1831, still under the spell of that event.

Though it is one of his smallest paintings, it is of the utmost significance stylistically, displaying a remarkably impressionistic quality, suggesting, vaguely, rather than supplying realistic detail. It is instructive to compare Delacroix's painting with the well-known drawing by Ingres (Rome, April or May 1819) which represents the musician in a composed, quiet, stately way, his general appearance being quite placid. Delacroix draws attention to Paganini's face—yellowish, with a trancelike expression that was often noted by observers—and to his hands. These dominate the picture, yet neither hands nor face, nor his violin, are drawn with any precision. There is a little brightness in the foreground, as from a footlight. It has been said that Paganini liked to perform on a dark stage illuminated by a single candle placed at his feet, casting ghostly

Niccolò Paganini *by Eugène Delacroix (1831?), oil on cardboard panel, 49 × 28 cm, The Phillips Collection, Washington, D.C.*

shadows. Delacroix creates the same atmosphere by providing the highlights mentioned above which contrast with the almost total darkness of the background. The painting also hints at the player's peculiar stance—contorted; twisted at the hips. Again eyewitness accounts corroborate that this was his characteristic playing position.

Given the virtuoso's fame and notoriety it is not surprising that some drawings and paintings dwell on the sensational aspects of his public appearances. A silhouette by Edouard shows him playing a violin with one string, a feat with which he inevitably amazed audiences. Though he often improvised, he also composed a number of pieces to be played on the G-string alone. Other portraits show him wearing decorations: such honors bestowed on an artist were a matter of great prestige. Like Mozart, Paganini was entitled to wear the Papal Order of the Golden Spur.

Performing on one string and other dazzling tricks show only one side of his musical personality. Among his compositions, the *Twenty-Four Caprices* for violin alone represent a milestone in the development of violin technique. Moreover, some of the century's foremost composers were inspired to write works of their own, based on themes from the *Caprices*. Liszt, Czerny, Schumann, and Brahms were among them.

The memories of Paganini's Paris concerts remained with Delacroix. Many years later, after attending a concert by the violin virtuoso Ernst, Delacroix noted in his journal that Ernst's playing reminded him of Paganini, whose works contain difficulties that "still make most of them impossible for even the most brilliant violinists. Here is the true inventor, the man with a natural genius for his art" (Wellington, 309).

Charcoal drawing of Niccolò Paganini by J. A. D. Ingres, 1819. Musée du Louvre, Paris

Niccolò Paganini playing a violin with one string. Silhouette by Albert Edouard

Gioacchino Rossini

It is hard for us today to imagine the tremendous popularity of some of the great composers from the early and mid-nineteenth century. Even among today's rock music stars it may be difficult to find examples of public adulation such as was accorded to Rossini, Liszt, and a few of their contemporaries.

Called "The Swan of Pesaro," Gioacchino Rossini (1792-1868) still remains that city's greatest son. Like Mozart, Rossini wrote some attractive pieces before he reached his teens. He was commissioned to write an opera for Venice before he was twenty. From then on, light and serious operas flowed from his pen with ease and speed: forty operas in twenty years, six operas in the year 1812 alone. Writing *The Barber of Seville* occupied him less than a month, perhaps a mere two weeks. Though a fiasco at its opening night, it soon became a rousing and lasting success. Indeed, the *Barber* may be the world's most performed opera.

Ary Scheffer (1795–1858) was of German and Dutch ancestry. After the death of his father in 1811, young Ary was taken to Paris where he continued his studies. He began exhibiting at the Salon in 1812. At the home of General Lafayette he met many members of the French nobility, including the duke and duchess of Orléans, the future king and queen of France. By 1826, Scheffer moved freely in their household, instructed their children, and received many commissions for paintings. The friendship continued after the duke's ascent to the throne in 1830. Scheffer's position was fortunate; being close to the king he was invited to contribute many portraits to the gallery in Versailles. He continued to exhibit at the Paris Salon until 1855. His reputation was that of a talented painter, though not one of the truly great, and of a kind, sincere person. In spite of his ties to the court he seems to have harbored liberal political opinions, causing him to remark that, like Lafayette, he should go to America "where to think was not a crime" (Hubbard, 337).

Scheffer was fond of music. Some of Paris' outstanding musicians sang and played in his atelier. According to E. W. Six, he was on friendly terms with Chopin, Liszt, and Gounod, whom he painted in 1830, 1839, and 1855 respectively.

We cannot verify the claim by Waagen that he had seen a Rossini portrait in Scheffer's studio during the 1830s. It is known, however, that in

Title page of the piano score of Rossini's opera **Adelaide di Borgogna,** *with illustration by Moritz von Schwind*

Gioacchino Rossini *by Ary Scheffer (1843), oil on canvas, 64 × 54 cm, Conservatoire National Supérieur de Musique, Paris*

1843, Rossini returned to Paris from Bologna, chiefly to consult physicians. On the way he had stopped in Parma where Verdi, later to become famous himself, called on him. Rossini arrived in Paris on May 27 and stayed for four months. During this period the great man and his wife were visited by "over 2,000 people—musicians, writers, diplomats, painters, and other prominent Parisians and foreigners" (Weinstock, 230). It was during this stay that Scheffer portrayed the master.

In this oil painting Rossini looks into the distance with a serious but animated expression. It is a formal pose, typical of much portraiture of the age, with his left hand tucked under his coat. His face and hands stand out against a dark background. Scheffer's signature and the date are barely visible at right.

The portrait (which, after many unsuccessful efforts, we located at the Paris Conservatoire) served as the model for several engravings and lithographs; along with other portraits these are preserved in the extensive collection of Rossiniana housed in the Casa Rossini in the composer's native town.

Rossini's earlier triumphs had taken him through much of Europe. Vienna had succumbed to a veritable Rossini mania by the time the composer arrived there in 1822. His visit with Beethoven was somewhat strained, not only because of Beethoven's deafness, but because he was quite aware that the Viennese were more charmed by the Italian's melodies than by Beethoven's own opera, *Fidelio*.

Rossini's great vogue in Vienna is reflected in the many editions of his music published there at this time, 1822-1825. Of special interest to us is a group of piano scores of popular Rossini operas for which the painter Moritz von Schwind (see below, p. 75) supplied attractive title page illustrations.

A fair number of Rossini portraits has been preserved—not surprising in view of his fame. By his time, photography had become an accepted medium for portraiture, and several photographs of Rossini in his later life have

Rossini, Berlioz, and Wagner. Caricature by Honoré Daumier, 1856

become well known. "Rossini" was a good name: it seems likely today that at least one portrait by a famous artist, previously considered to represent the composer, is not authentic. This is a drawing by Ingres, dated Rome, 1819, which for more than 100 years has been considered, by Ingres specialists and musicians, to be "a beautiful portrait of the musician" (Naef, vol. 2, 339–340). Recently Hans Naef has produced evidence that the person portrayed is one Giovanni Rosini, an Italian novelist and critic, and that the attribution to Rossini came about because of the similarity of names.

There are references to a Rossini portrait by Delacroix (Wessling) which we have been unable to locate. Delacroix had attended Paris performances of Rossini's *Otello*, in 1821 and again in 1847. At the latter date he was working on his painting *Othello and Desdemona*.

A Rossini statue by Antoine Etex for some time adorned the foyer of the Paris Opéra. Funds had been raised for this purpose by a committee which included the composers Donizetti and Meyerbeer, along with Ary Scheffer. The poet Heine, with his customary wit, claimed that Meyerbeer always took great pains not to walk by it.

Among the many caricatures of Rossini there is one, little known, by Honoré Daumier (1808–1879), one of France's great graphic artists. The lithograph shows (l. to r.) Berlioz, Wagner, and Rossini as wine merchant, grocer, and butcher respectively. In Daumier's caption they say (Wagner:) "To say that from now on we must give honest weight . . . (Rossini:) cannot foist off bones as meat . . . (Berlioz:) must sell wine that really is wine . . . (in chorus:) HOW REVOLTING!" Daumier's caricature appeared in the satirical journal *Charivari* on January 10, 1856. Its significance (it refers to a recent scandal at the Opéra) is discussed by Bischoff.

On the day after Rossini's death (November 13, 1868), Gustave Doré sketched the composer on his deathbed. His painting of the following year was based on the earlier sketch.

Franz Schubert

"Schubert is dead! With him we have lost our most serene friend, our most cherished treasure!" The painter Moritz von Schwind (1804–1871) expressed his heartfelt grief when he received word of the composer's death which had occurred on November 19, 1828. By that time the young Schwind had left his native Vienna for Munich, where he embarked on what was to be a highly successful career. Eventually he became one of the best known romantic painters in the German-speaking world.

Although Schwind did not leave us any large, formal painting of his friend Franz Schubert (1797–1828), he did portray him in a surprising number of paintings and drawings. Sometimes Schubert appears prominently, sometimes virtually hidden—as in this painting, *A Symphony*, in which he appears third from the left in the back.

Schwind's association with the composer, moreover, was unusually close. Much has been written about Schubert and his circle of friends—that group of (mostly young) musicians, writers, and painters that became rather famous for their frequent gatherings which they called "Schubertiads." They would discuss art, literature, philosophy; also politics, though probably cautiously, given the watchful eye of the government during the Metternich era. The get-togethers were social as well: one would eat and drink, dance, play parlor games, and go on excursions in the country.

Throughout life Schwind remembered these occasions with nostalgia. In a letter to Franz von Schober he refers to "these beautiful, unforgettable years" (Kobald, 132). The fond memories inspired a number of paintings and drawings, no doubt somewhat idealized, in which Schubert is included.

While some of these were done after Schubert's death, others date from their years together, such as the small likeness of the composer in an etching, *A Ball Game at Atzenbrugg*, c. 1820. It shows the "Schubertians" at play, one of them playing the violin, with Schubert sitting on the grass, smoking a pipe. Another Schwind oil painting, *A Walk Before the Town Gate*, was done shortly before the painter moved to Munich. Those walking include Schubert, the singer Johann Michael Vogl, the painter Schober, and others of the circle. Schwind included himself in this and other paintings.

A Schubert Evening at Joseph von Spaun's is one of the nostalgic pieces, done in 1868. More than forty of the guests represented in this sepia drawing have been identified, with Schubert in the center, at the piano, next to Vogl and Spaun. The latter was among Schubert's most devoted friends.

One of Schwind's great satisfactions late in life was the commission he received to paint the frescoes for the new opera house in Vienna. (They are still there today, in spite of the near-destruction of the building in 1945.) Among the subjects Schwind included are scenes from the Schubert songs *Erlkönig* and *Der Fischer*.

Our painting's title, *A Symphony*, actually applies to only one panel of the large painting, a panel such as we find in medieval and Renaissance altarpieces. Schwind had thought out quite an elaborate scenario which he described in letters of 1849 and 1850 to his friend, the musician Schädl. *A Symphony* represents a performance of Beethoven's Fantasy for Piano, Chorus, and Orchestra, Op. 80. Some of the many singers and players can be identified; possibly everyone included in the painting was known to Schwind and his friends. Again Schubert, in the lower left group of singers, is partially hidden, and again Schwind painted himself into his picture, here turning pages for the pianist, Maximiliana Brentano, to whom Beethoven had dedicated his Piano Sonata, Op. 109. Schubert's friend Franz Lachner is conducting, Vogl and another friend, Franz von Schober, are depicted, along with a Fräulein Hetzenecker, the vocal soloist (front left, standing, holding music; this last attribution according to Karl Kobald).

Since the painting was intended to be an homage to Beethoven, that composer's bust, crowned with laurel, is prominently displayed in the painting's exact center. In all, this is an attractive genre painting, in a Biedermeier setting. In the tradition of pictorial homage it recalls Ingres's *Apotheosis of Homer* (1827; second version 1865), in which, at Homer's feet, many seventeenth and eighteenth-century artists are included, among them Shakespeare, Molière, the painter David, and the composer Gluck.

Is this very small Schubert portrait a good likeness of the composer? It would seem so, if we compare it with Schwind's other Schubert portraits, and if we compare these with the well-known watercolor (later also an oil painting) by W. A. Rieder (1796–1880), done from life and considered particularly lifelike by Schwind himself. We also have corroboration in descriptions of Schubert's general appearance. Though they disagree in some details they remark on the unassuming impression he made, on his round, somewhat puffy face, his curly hair and bushy eyebrows, his nearsightedness that caused him to wear glasses all the time, according to his friend Anselm Hüttenbrenner even while asleep. There also is agreement that his placid

A Symphony *by Moritz von Schwind (1852), oil on canvas, one panel of a larger (166 × 99 cm) painting, Neue Pinakothek, Munich*

expression would change totally as soon as he became involved in music making or lively conversation.

During his lifetime Schubert was not widely known. By 1828 few of his works had been performed in public concerts, and of his more-than–600 songs, only about 100 had been published. Ten years later Robert Schumann, on a pilgrimage to Vienna, visited Schubert's grave and met his brother Ferdinand. Schumann's subsequent essays on Schubert's music (published in the journal *Neue Zeitschrift für Musik,* founded by Schumann in 1833) did much to bring Schubert's work to the attention of the musical world at large.

Hector Berlioz

Courbet's painting of Berlioz tells us much about the composer and his personality, affected by a life that had been tempestuous in both its personal and professional aspects.

Hector Berlioz (1803–1869) was a major composer of the mid-nineteenth century. In many ways he was ahead of his time; he therefore was attacked by many who could not understand the boldness of his new musical ideas, especially as they pertained to harmony and orchestration. Other contemporaries were enthusiastic about this French composer who was so closely associated with the stormy, rebellious aspects of romanticism in all the arts.

Hector Berlioz conducting a "monster concert." Caricature by Gustave Doré, 1850

Berlioz, like other musicians of the age, also expressed himself through the written word, chiefly through contributions to newspapers and periodicals. Musical journalism had begun to flourish in France. Berlioz's feuilletons often were witty and sarcastic; by the same token his own music, some of it conceived on a startlingly grand scale, became the subject of sarcastic commentary, both verbal and pictorial. Caricatures by Daumier, Doré, and others attest to the controversial nature of some of Berlioz's work. "Monster concerts," such as those given by Berlioz in connection with the Paris Exhibition of 1855, invited this kind of fun-poking, as in Doré's drawing shown here. (Courbet attended one of these concerts.) Berlioz, to be sure, had his own reservations about the occasions, and is said to have complained, "All of Paris wants to sing, blow, and scrape." One such outdoor concert involved the participation of 200 drums.

Though fame came to Berlioz eventually, much of his life consisted of a struggle for recognition, of frustration due to indifference in high places. He was forever trying to train musicians to understand his intentions, to execute his music which at times was far beyond their comprehension.

We are fortunate to have a portrait of Berlioz by an artist of Courbet's stature. Another portrait, formerly attributed to Daumier, is now believed to be a copy by André Gill of a photograph by Nadar, one of the nineteenth-century pioneers of artistic photography, especially portraiture. Though Delacroix may have planned to limn a Berlioz portrait, nothing came of it.

Ever since his childhood, Gustave Courbet (1819–1877) had demonstrated an interest in, if no special talent for, music. Two of his several self portraits picture him as a musician: *The Guitar Player*, submitted for exhibition in 1845, and *The Cellist* (1851). Neither is considered to be among his major works—the cellist, for some reason, is left-handed. Official recognition came to Courbet soon after this, but some paintings, intended for showing at the International Exhibition of 1855, again were rejected. Like Berlioz, Courbet was a fighter and in some ways a revolutionary. Having been excluded from the 1855 show, he arranged for an exhibit of his own and published his artistic manifesto, its main tenet being: picture life as it really is. Courbet's later involvement in politics culminated in his participation in the Paris Commune, during and after the Franco-Prussian War of 1870–71. His alleged responsibility for the demolition of the Vendôme Column (he considered it a monument to French imperialism, out of place in the Rue de la Paix [peace]) led to his arrest, trial, and prison sentence. He died in exile in Switzerland.

Courbet had met Berlioz in 1850 or earlier, through the painter's lifelong friend Francis Wey who was anxious for Courbet to do portraits of some well-known individuals. Berlioz agreed to sit for the painter—reluctantly, probably as a favor to Wey. Things did not go well:

[Courbet] had a mania for singing songs in his own way, without rhyming the words or keeping any rhythm. . . . These formless melodies he presumed to bawl out to Berlioz while he painted. At first Berlioz thought that he was being made fun of; then, seeing that this was not the case, he took Courbet for an idiot. And as he understood absolutely nothing about painting, he let himself be convinced . . . that the portrait was worthless. (Charles Léger, quoted by Lindsay, 74–75)

Courbet, unhappy with the whole affair, wanted to give the portrait to Wey, who turned it down. It is now in the Louvre.

A less-than-happy encounter, then, between painter and composer, yet it resulted in a major painting. For one thing, it is a good likeness of Berlioz, to judge by the 1867 photograph; for another, it is an outstanding example of Courbet's mastery—his best portrait, in the opinion of experts. The composer's mien is serious, somewhat suspicious, even angry. Dark shadows and a dark background, with little detail except for the facial features, emphasize the mood. Such concentration on the face is also found in other Courbet portraits from the 1850s. An oil sketch of our portrait (c. 1849) is reproduced in T. J. Clark's study.

Hector Berlioz *by Gustave Courbet (c. 1850), oil on canvas, 61 × 48 cm, Musée du Louvre, Paris*

Mikhail Glinka

The writer and critic Vladimir Stasov advocated the music of Mikhail Glinka (1804–1857) to members of "the Five": Balakirev, Borodin, Cui, Mussorgski (p. 100), and Rimsky-Korsakov (p. 110). The group was especially drawn to the harmonic and rhythmic devices Glinka incorporated in *A Life for the Czar* and *Ruslan and Ludmila*. There was, as well, the use of distinctive Russian historical and literary materials that made him an inspiration for this loose alliance of younger composers.

It was at Stasov's, where members of the group occasionally got together, that Ilya Repin (1844–1930) met the Five. Shortly after Repin came into their circle, he was given a commission by a St. Petersburg hotel owner to paint a group portrait of Slavic composers. Featured among them were to be Chopin, Glinka, and Smetana. At that time Glinka had been dead almost fifteen years, so Repin had to work from photographs.

The portrait shown here is also based, at least in conception, on an 1871 preparatory drawing Repin made of the group portrait of Slavic composers. Already in this preliminary sketch, Glinka is shown reclining, pen to mouth, supposedly in the process of composing *Ruslan and Ludmila*. Masterful touches, however, have been added in the final painting. Only hinted at in the drawing, the nightstand now serves as a bold introductory device, leading from the left. The manuscript on the table reinforces this diagonal. Along with the pillow, this open volume serves to frame the composer's head. On the right-hand side of the portrait, his legs are put to the same compositional purpose as the nightstand and manuscript. These various compositional gestures create an atmosphere of unposed inspiration.

Only in Paris, where Repin lived from 1873 to 1876, could the artist have learned to compose portraits in which so much space was used to give so little specific information about his sitter. It took almost ten years for the lessons of Paris to bear fruit in Repin's work. Here, the nonchalance of the pose and brushwork reflects the influence of impressionism. The sophisticated compositional use to which the lower half of the painting is put also shows Repin's knowledge of the early work of Edgar Degas.

While clearly representing Glinka in spirit, the portrait only vaguely resembles photographs of the composer. Rather obviously, Repin has chosen to glorify Mikhail Glinka, founder of the Russian nationalist school, the same way Glinka himself glorified the music of his native land. When Glinka first arrived in St. Petersburg in 1817, the city was both the political and cultural capital of Russia. Built on Western ideals, St. Petersburg boasted a musical life no less brilliant than that found in many large cities in western Europe. Italian and French opera formed the dominant feature of musical activity in the capital. Russian opera (that was written by native composers on Russian librettos) did not exist as such. Glinka was to change all that, but only after a fifteen-year apprenticeship to the music of Cherubini, Mozart, and Rossini.

He spent the last three of those years, 1830–33, primarily in Milan, where he came to know both Bellini and Donizetti. Most of the compositions Glinka wrote while in Italy took the form of piano variations (*à la* Liszt) on themes from operas by his Italian friends. Certain features of Italian opera definitely appealed to the composer, but they also convinced him that he could never master Italian sentiment. Even before leaving that country, Glinka had begun to use Russian folk songs as the dominant thematic material for his compositions of 1833–34.

Almost immediately upon his return to St. Petersburg, Glinka set to work on *A Life for the Czar*, the first of the two operas for which he is chiefly remembered. Based on a Russian story about events from the life of Czar Nicholas I, *A Life* incorporated both Russian history and, once again, melodic material derived from Russian folk song. The latter was sufficiently varied to be assimilated into the score without being obvious. The opera was first performed in 1836. Accounts of its reception vary, but reaction was enthusiastic enough to encourage Glinka to write a second opera the following year. Based on a poem by Pushkin, *Ruslan and Ludmila* featured a set of Russian ideas similar to those found in *A Life for the Czar*. One of the Five, Balakirev, successfully conducted the first performance of Glinka's *Ruslan* outside of Russia. This production, mounted by the Czech Opera in Prague ten years after the composer's death, assured Glinka's fame outside his native land. For once, it reversed the process of importing European operas, so entrenched in the St. Petersburg of Glinka's youth, and exported a native Russian opera to the West.

Mikhail Glinka Composing "Ruslan and Ludmila"
by Ilya Repin (1887), oil on canvas, 98 × 117 cm,
Tretyakov Gallery, Moscow

Felix Mendelssohn-Bartholdy

"It is fearful. It is mad. I am quite giddy and confused. London is the grandest and most complicated monster on the face of the earth." Thus wrote Felix Mendelssohn (1809–1847) in the first letter to his family after arriving in London in April 1829 (Mendelssohn, 45). Only twenty when he made this first trip to England, he would visit Great Britain nine more times in the eighteen years he had yet to live.

From the first, Mendelssohn was captivated by the pace, the style, and the women of England. His letters and the portrait by Warren Childe (1778–1862) show how quickly the composer adopted British manners and dress. Childe's three-quarter-length portrait is tightly, almost dryly, executed, rendering in considerable detail the clothing worn by Mendelssohn. In his right hand he holds a top cap, virtually mandatory for a man of fashion in England in the 1820s. He wears a fashionable dark dress coat, cravat, and lighter-colored waistcoat with watch chain.

In fact, his clothing in this portrait appears to be that worn by Mendelssohn on the second of his concerts in London. On that occasion, he appeared in the Argyle Room where he performed the Weber *Konzertstück in F Minor*, Sir George Smart directing. The young Felix would report of that concert to his family, in a letter written June 7, 1829, "I remained in good spirits and changed into my dress clothes (for Becky's journal of fashions: very long white trousers, brown silk waistcoat, black necktie and blue dress coat)" (Mendelssohn, 50).

Mendelssohn made no fewer than six concert appearances in London in the same number of weeks. While these performances did not result in the financial success he might have wanted, he did get a chance to present his overture to *A Midsummer Night's Dream* to receptive British audiences. Judging from the enthusiastic response that greeted this piece, and his concerts in general, it seems that Londoners were as enthusiastic about Mendelssohn's music as the young musician was about their city.

While in London, the composer had the opportunity to see the gifted Maria Malibran as Desdemona in Rossini's (see pp. 70ff.) *Otello*. Even though Mendelssohn had minor reservations about her performance, he was taken by Malibran's acting and her "fire and power" (Mendelssohn, 46). Like Warren Childe, Malibran herself was a miniaturist and, in 1833, painted two small portraits of Vincenzo Bellini, now in the Museo Belliniano, Catania.

In late July, Mendelssohn left London for Edinburgh, where he gave no public concerts. For pleasure, he traveled to such places as Glasgow, Inverness, Abbotsford, the Highlands, and the Hebrides. While visiting the ruins of the Chapel of Mary Stuart in Edinburgh, he first decided to write his *Scotch Symphony*, not completed until twelve years later. There was, however, a much more immediate musical consequence of that trip to Scotland. The same year, 1829, he wrote *Die einsame Insel*, to be revised a year later under the title *The Hebrides*, or *Fingal's Cave*, his most popular composition since *Midsummer Night's Dream* (1826).

While in Scotland Mendelssohn also drew a variety of charming sketches of various locations he visited. These drawings are now in the Bodleian Library, Oxford. Primarily self-taught, Mendelssohn received semiformal training in drawing and watercolor on at least two separate occasions in his life.

A sketchbook was his constant companion on his travels. He carried one, not just on this, his only visit to Scotland, but on later trips through Europe, particularly to picturesque locations. As one might expect of a musician given to intelligible form, he felt most comfortable when treating architecture. In these studies, his use of line is secure; his mastery of perspective remains somewhat forced, but appealing. While always carefully composed, his landscapes are fresh, sometimes revealing novel solutions in their treatment of atmosphere and distance. Only when working with figures does the talented composer-artist seem ill-at-ease.

In contrast, the human figure, and particularly, the face, provided the focus of Warren Childe's art. A member of the Royal Academy and the Society of British Artists, he specialized in miniatures of British actors and actresses. Perhaps theater provided the forum through which Mendelssohn, a visitor to London, gained his introduction to Childe.

Felix Mendelssohn-Bartholdy by Warren Childe (1829), watercolor, 21 × 16.8 cm, Mendelssohn-Archiv, Staatsbibliothek, Preussischer Kulturbesitz, Berlin

81

Frédéric Chopin

Here we have an outstanding example of collaboration between two major artists: one of the foremost romantic painters portrayed one of the age's greatest, most universally loved composers. Given their fame it is not surprising that much has been written about both of them—their lives, their ideas, their art. Thus we also know much about the history of this painting.

Eugène Delacroix (1798–1863) was born near Paris and died there. During his lifetime French romanticism saw its greatest flourishing in painting, literature, and music. Paris, then even more than now, was a center (probably the most important center in Europe) of artistic activity, much of it stimulated by interaction, by exchanges of ideas between artists in several fields. Musicians were inspired by literature and philosophy; painters and playwrights attended concerts. There were close friendships among artists and, of course, opposing factions on many issues, artistic and also political ones.

It is significant for our purpose that Delacroix, from his early childhood on, was fond of music; he seriously studied several instruments. Music was a constant source of inspiration to him as a painter. He was happy when he could paint in a church, listening to the organ and choir. "Music puts me into a state of exaltation that is favorable to painting" (Huyghe, 197). Interrelationships or parallels between the arts of painting and music occupied his mind frequently; such thoughts have been preserved in many entries in his journal, including the very last entry, less than two months before his death, in which he compares looking at paintings and listening to music.

Delacroix's special fondness for Mozart's music is well documented. One editor of his journal has pointed out that Mozart is mentioned more often than any other artist in any field except Rubens. His thoughts in many instances were kindled by what he heard. He avidly attended concerts and opera and was in contact, at musical soirees or elsewhere, with leading musicians of his time, including Rossini and Gounod.

The life story of Chopin (1810–1849) has often been told, factually or as sentimentalized fiction. Chopin's liaison with George Sand constitutes a specially romantic chapter of his life; it also figures in the history of our portrait, for Delacroix had met Chopin through her. In her *Histoire de ma vie*, she calls the painter "one of my best friends among the world of artists, . . . a daring innovator" (p. 243). She admires his colors but finds it difficult to describe them in words. "Can one describe Mozart's *Requiem?*"

Her account of Delacroix's personality and physical appearance ("pale, fragile, nervous, complaining of a thousand little infirmities") reminds us, in a startling way, of what we know of Chopin, from Delacroix's portrait.

Sand, in her *Impressions et souvenirs*, compares the two artists, both very dear to her: Chopin was "a musician, nothing but a musician. . . . He has plenty of wit, irony, subtlety, but he cannot understand painting and sculpture at all," while "Delacroix, who is more varied in his gifts, appreciates music; . . . his taste is sure and exquisite" (Huyghe, 194).

Delacroix repeatedly stayed with the remarkable couple at Sand's country mansion, Nohant; on warm summer days and nights he found life there very pleasant. "Now and then there come to you through the window opening on the garden, whiffs of the music of Chopin, who is working in his room; this mingles with the song of the nightingales and the odor of the roses" (Niecks, vol. 2, 129).

Chopin also was happy with the painter's company. "He is the most admirable artist possible—I have spent delightful times with him. He adores Mozart, knows all his operas by heart" (Letter to Franchomme; Niecks, vol. 2, 120). In 1838, during one of his stays at Nohant, Delacroix painted Sand, standing next to Chopin, who sits at the piano. A sketch of this double portrait has been preserved in the Louvre. Later, possibly for financial reasons, the finished work was divided into two canvases. The George Sand portion now is in Copenhagen.

Thus our painting of the composer actually is half of that double portrait. How true to life it is can be gathered from several accounts of the time. Once more we hear from George Sand: "His face has the beauty of a sad woman . . . pure and slender of form, . . . an expression at once tender and severe, chaste and passionate" (Cortot, 7). And Franz Liszt:

His appearance formed a harmonious whole; . . . his blue eyes were more spiritual than dreamy, his gentle, delicate smile held no trace of bitterness. The fineness and transparency of his complexion bewitched the eye, his fair hair was silky, his carriage distinguished. . . . His gestures were full of grace and freedom. (Cortot, 8)

And finally, a description of the portrait by someone who knew it well: Antoine-François Marmontel, pianist and composer:

This is the Chopin of the last years, ailing, broken by suffering, already marked by death. . . . The attenuated and lengthened features are strongly accentuated . . . but the lines of the countenance remain beautiful; the oval of the face, the aquiline

Frédéric Chopin *by Eugène Delacroix (1838), oil on canvas, 45 × 37 cm, Musée du Louvre, Paris*

nose and its harmonious curve, give to this sickly physiognomy the stamp of poetic distinction peculiar to Chopin. (Quoted by Niecks, vol. 2, 329)

To realize the esteem in which Chopin was held in Paris one might turn to the account of his funeral, as given by Niecks. It provides a vivid picture of the elaborate services held in the Church of the Madeleine, including a performance of Mozart's *Requiem* (Chopin, too, was very fond of Mozart) and some of Chopin's own music, arranged for orchestra. Liszt, Meyerbeer,

and Delacroix were among the many artists who took part in the ceremonies, along with high public officials. Delacroix then headed a committee formed to have a monument erected in honor of the deceased; it was unveiled, at the graveside, a year after the composer's death.

Also after Chopin's death (according to some biographers), Delacroix made a pencil sketch of his friend, with a laurel crown and a cape, suggesting the costume of Dante. Below the image we read but two words: "Cher Chopin." The sketch today is in the Louvre.

Robert Schumann

Compared to earlier portraits of Robert Schumann (1810–1856) by other artists, this one by J.-J.-B. Laurens (1801–1890) shows the composer physically transformed. The changes reflected Schumann's growing mental illness late in life. The artist himself remarked on the enlargement of his subject's eyes. Schumann's face, always full, here appears swollen. Yet this is not an unflattering portrait. The firmness of the composer's lips and the clarity of his eyes indicate an admirable intelligence. Sensitive shading in chalk around the temples, cheeks, and jaw lends a certain warmth to the last portrait made of Schumann before his death.

On a separate sheet added to the bottom of the drawing is an inscription: "In memory and appreciation (*Zum Andenken in Werthschätzung*), Robert Schumann." Above, Schumann wrote out the first four bars of the violin melody in the third movement of his D minor Trio. Laurens, who was a friend of the Schumanns, corresponded with them for three years and received two other signed compositions from the German master: the celebrated Piano Quintet, Op. 44; and the Sonata No. 2 for Piano and Violin, Op. 121.

J.-J.-B. Laurens was a gifted polymath who succeeded at virtually everything he tried. He studied science, music, art, and archaeology. Born in Carpentras, Laurens worked there as the secretary of the School of Medicine, and as church organist. From all accounts, he was a gifted musician, playing also the violin, cello, and piano.

So enamoured was Laurens with music that he sought out leading composers of his time. He met and got to know Liszt, Mendelssohn, Rossini, Auber, Chopin, and Thomas. He made portraits of these latter three, plus Brahms (see pp. 98f.), Gounod, Mendelssohn's daughters, Saint-Saëns, and Clara and Robert Schumann.

An inveterate traveler, Laurens had stopped to visit Schumann while in Düsseldorf in October 1853. The peripatetic French musician and artist could hardly have realized that he had arrived during the great romantic composer's last truly productive month, begun with the completion of the Violin Concerto in D. This piece was written for the young virtuoso Joseph Joachim, who encouraged Brahms to visit Schumann at the same time Laurens was in Düsseldorf. While some of the harmonic complexities of Schumann's final works presage Wagner, the compositions of this period generally eschewed the lyricism and expressiveness that made Schumann a leading figure of the romantic movement.

Signs of Robert Schumann's growing mental deterioration became evident soon after Laurens and Brahms departed Düsseldorf. Before the end of October, Schumann, who served as Düsseldorf's municipal director of music, was partially relieved of his conducting responsibilities because he started to lose his place in the music and could not maintain discipline in the orchestra. For a time Robert Schumann seemed to weather these problems. He and Clara made a triumphal concert tour of northern Europe, which concluded in January 1854.

The month of February saw Schumann's mental health decline even further. He experienced disturbances in which angels (and subsequently devils) appeared to him. He attempted to drown himself in the Rhine and voluntarily had himself placed in an asylum at Endenich (near Bonn) early in March of that year. The diagnosis of this mental disorder is uncertain—perhaps syphilis. Schumann would die at Endenich on September 29, 1856.

Robert Schumann *by Jean-Joseph-Bonaventure Laurens (1853), pencil, 30 × 20 cm, silverpoint on paper, Bibliothèque Inguimbertine, Carpentras, France*

Franz Liszt

Franz (Ferenc) Liszt (1811–1886) is among the most frequently portrayed composers of his era. His splendid career as a pianist and composer, and his flamboyant lifestyle and its romantic aspects, may explain this.

As a Liszt portrait, Danhauser's painting is somewhat similar to Schwind's canvas (*A Symphony*, p. 75) in which Schubert appears as one of many identifiable persons. Danhauser, by showing Liszt in a characteristic pose and setting, tells us much about the artistic world in which the famous pianist-composer lived. To be sure, in this painting Liszt is the center of attention.

Liszt very much was part of the artistic milieu of Paris in the early nineteenth century, in which so many masterpieces of art, music, and literature were born. The social institution of the salon was just as conducive to this flourishing of the arts as were museum, concert hall, or theater. New art works and new ideas were often discussed and tried out in this more intimate setting before they reached a larger audience. At times such gatherings took place in the homes of the artists themselves. Liszt remembered a soiree at Chopin's quarters, though one wonders whether there would have been room for all those he mentions—Heine, Meyerbeer, the singer Nourrit, George Sand, and Delacroix among them, as well as Liszt and his amour, Countess d'Agoult. Chopin's biographer Nieck points out that large gatherings were more typical of Liszt's lifestyle than Chopin's.

Joseph Danhauser (b. Vienna 1805; d. there 1845) was best known for informal genre pictures such as this one—informal as opposed to conventional, posed portraits. He had an interest in music, played the violin well, and was a member of Schubert's circle. Liszt, while in Vienna in 1840, acquired Danhauser's death mask of Beethoven.

Franz Liszt at the Piano or *A Soiree at Franz Liszt's* also dates from 1840. Those represented on this canvas suggest that the setting is Paris; most likely it therefore was not done from life. Danhauser must have been familiar with Liszt's Paris environment. In the painting we see (l. to r.) Alexandre Dumas *père*, Victor Hugo, George Sand, Paganini, Rossini, and Marie d'Agoult. On the wall is Byron's portrait, on the piano a bust of Beethoven (compare Schwind's *A Symphony*). The grand piano clearly displays the name of Conrad Graf, the Viennese instrument maker who had commissioned the painting! Elaine Brody's detailed 1983 study of the painting led her to the conclusion that not all

those portrayed could have been in Paris at the same time—but how are all these admiring listeners related to Liszt?

Alexandre Dumas, the father, (1802–1870) achieved great popularity with his historical novels *The Three Musketeers* (1844) and *The Count of Monte Cristo* (1845). He moved in the Paris circles frequented by Liszt, including the salon of Princess Cristina Belgiojoso. It was she who in 1837 arranged the famous pianistic "duel" between Liszt and Thalberg, a musical contest that attracted a large, admission-paying audience.

As a playwright, **Victor Hugo** (1802–1885) was more closely involved with the ascent of romanticism in France than anyone else. His play *Hernani* (1830) in particular was controversial in its flouting of long-established dramatic conventions. The writer's friend Delacroix and the composer Berlioz are said to have been among those in the audience. Hugo took part in the musical life of Paris. He attended Paganini's first Paris recital, and he often saw Liszt during this revolutionary period. Bellini, Donizetti, Verdi, Liszt, and countless other nineteenth-century composers found inspiration in Hugo's literary works.

We have already considered the place of **George Sand** in the Chopin-Liszt circle. Liszt at various times had stayed at Nohant, Sand's country home. He found the setting congenial and conducive to his studies of Beethoven symphonies, all of which he eventually arranged for piano. In our painting Sand seems to wear male attire, as she frequently did. Nor did Danhauser forget that she was fond of smoking cigars.

Liszt's enormous admiration for **Paganini** showed itself in many ways. Paganini's *24 Caprices* inspired Liszt to transcribe five of them for piano. He included them in his six *Etudes d'exécution transcendante d'après Paganini* (1838), the sixth being a fantasy on *La campanella*, taken from Paganini's Violin Concerto in B Minor. The revised version of 1851 was entitled *Grandes Etudes de Paganini*. Liszt also wrote some essays about Paganini, including the obituary published in 1840. Liszt predicted that there will never be another Paganini, but also expressed hope that future artists will consider virtuosity a means, but not an end.

Before Danhauser painted his picture, **Rossini** had lived comfortably in Paris for some time. He wrote *Guillaume Tell* (1829) for the Paris Opéra; it was a stupendous success. His friendship with Liszt was established at this time. Their paths crossed again in 1837 in Milan where Rossini was then living—fond as always of giving parties that were famous for the host's outstanding cuisine. Eventually Liszt was invited to partici-

pate in these soirees. He showed his appreciation by providing and performing piano transcriptions of a group of twelve songs which Rossini had recently composed. Ricordi in Milan published them in 1838 as *Transcriptions des Soirées musicales de Rossini*. Liszt paid further homage to the composer of *Guillaume Tell* with a transcription of the overture of that opera.

Many years later, shortly before his death, Liszt visited Rossini's grave in Paris. He stayed a long time, lost in thought and shedding tears.

To trace the long, romantic involvement of Liszt with **Countess Marie d'Agoult** clearly is out of place here. Liszt and the countess met in Paris in 1833: it was love at first sight. Much has been written about her, including much that is critical. Their liaison was often difficult and stormy. It occurred during an important period in Liszt's career; it is right that she is included in this group of friends and admirers.

Of those artists whose Liszt paintings,

drawings, and lithographs are preserved, Ingres is the best known today; his drawing of the young Liszt was done in 1839. It is inscribed to Marie d'Agoult.

There are other Liszt portraits by artists of major stature who had solid reputations in their own time. They include Ary Scheffer (1835; there are several versions) and Wilhelm von Kaulbach (1843). Kaulbach's canvas *Die Hunnenschlacht* (The battle of the Huns) inspired Liszt to write his symphonic poem with the same title.

Other significant Liszt portraits are those by Moritz von Schwind and I. J. Repin, the latter being known for his portraits of Glinka (see p. 79) and Mussorgski (see p. 101).

Danhauser's is not the only group portrait that includes Liszt: Franz Kriehuber's *A Matinée at Liszt's* (Vienna, 1846) also shows the master at the keyboard, surrounded by four admiring musicians.

Franz Liszt at the Piano *or* A Soiree at Franz Liszt's, *by Joseph Danhauser (1840), oil on wood, 119 × 167 cm, Bildarchiv Preussischer Kulturbesitz, Berlin*

Giuseppe Verdi

For this pastel, Giuseppe Verdi (1813–1901) is dressed in top hat, overcoat, and scarf. In *Orpheus at Eighty,* Vincent Sheean complained of this "dandification" of the unassuming composer. The artist, Giovanni Boldini (1842–1931), made his reputation painting members of French society. Certainly he was attempting to show Verdi here more as a wealthy Parisian than as an Italian of peasant origins. Verdi was a cultural and political hero of the painter, who has treated him with ultimate sympathy. Boldini enlivened his treatment of Verdi's face with traces of impressionistic color, and fused areas of the cheeks and beard with the softness of pastels. On the other hand, there is an authority, a sureness, in the artist's touch that leaves no doubt about the identity of the sitter: Giuseppe Verdi, himself the great musical portraitist of human subjects.

Verdi completed his *Aida* in 1870. Thoughts of a new opera, *Otello,* did not come to the great composer for ten years; actual composition didn't begin for almost fifteen. Verdi might never have written another new opera after age fifty-seven had it not been for the prospect of working, once again, with a text based on Shakespeare, whose dramas elicited greater enthusiasm from the Italian composer than those of any other playwright. It was Verdi's publisher and agent, Giulio Ricordi, who cleverly lured the composer out of virtual retirement. First Ricordi proposed *Otello.* Then, a year later, he forwarded Arrigo Boito's completed libretto, the finest Verdi had yet to work with.

Revisions on *Simone Boccanegra* and *Don Carlos,* plus restagings of both operas at La Scala, kept Verdi from work on *Otello* until early 1884. By October 1885, he had written the opera, completing the orchestration a year later, about the time Boldini created his portrait of Verdi. When *Otello* was first performed in February 1887, critics greeted it with cries of a "New Verdi." In *Otello,* the master had so skillfully integrated orchestral playing with recitative and expressive singing that the opera took on a virtually seamless, heightened dramatic quality. Because of these new features, Verdi was accused of adapting Wagnerian reforms to the needs of Italian opera. Of course, Verdi vehemently denied these charges.

According to an interview that appeared in *Le Figaro* on April 17, 1886, Verdi claimed to have come to Paris at the end of March of that year to order an overcoat from his tailor (for the coming summer, no doubt). In fact, he was there in search of a baritone with the acting ability, the stage cunning, and, above all, the proper voice to perform the role of Iago. He found his man in the vain but brilliant Victor Maurel, who created the part of the vengeful, conspiring ensign when *Otello* was first staged at La Scala.

While Verdi was in Paris, his friend and former pupil, Emanuele Muzio, persuaded Verdi to sit for his fellow countryman, Giovanni Boldini. Formerly, the artist had been a member of the *Macchiaioli,* a loose confederation of Italian artists who shared similar concerns of light and landscape painting with the French impressionists. Since 1871, Boldini had made his residence in Paris. There, while painting some impressionist landscapes, he gained his reputation making portraits of French celebrities. Among the notables to sit for the artist were the Countess Gabrielle De Rasty and the famous baritone, Jean-Baptiste Faure, who inaugurated the role of the Marquis de Posa in Verdi's *Don Carlos* at the Paris Opera in 1867.

Boldini actually made two portraits of Verdi. For the first, Muzio and Giuseppina, the composer's wife, had accompanied him to Boldini's studio in Paris. Their presence made the artist nervous. Then Verdi and Muzio talked business while Verdi sat for the portrait. These distractions disconcerted Boldini and left him unhappy with the final product. Seven years later, however, at the premier of *Falstaff,* Boldini presented the composer with this first portrait, which now resides in the Verdi Home for Musicians in Milan.

Because of his dissatisfaction with the initial portrait, the painter asked Verdi to sit a second time. Concerned with the orchestration and production of *Otello,* Verdi agreed only with reluctance. The first two hours of the sitting went so well, however, that Verdi played portions of his new score on the piano and ate lunch with the artist. He sat again that very afternoon, after which Boldini completed the pastel, which is inscribed at the top with the date "9 April 1886." The artist was so pleased with this version that he refused to sell it, though it was shown at both the Universal Exhibition of Paris in 1889 and the first Venice Biennale. In 1918, the painter presented the portrait to the Galleria Nazionale d'Arte Moderna in Rome.

For his part, Verdi was impressed enough with Boldini to present him with an autographed copy of the score of *Otello* after the artist attended the inaugural performances of the opera. The inscription read, "To an outstanding artist and my dearest friend, Boldini, Giuseppe Verdi, Milan, 9 February, 1887."

Giuseppe Verdi *by Giovanni Boldini (1886), pastel on cardboard, 65 × 54 cm, Galleria Nazionale d'Arte Moderna, Rome*

Richard Wagner

Since 1880, Richard Wagner (1813–1883) had been spending the majority of each year in southern Italy, primarily for reasons of health. Revived by the sun, he had taken up residence in the lavish Hotel des Palmes in Palermo in November 1881. While there he completed the last act of his final opera, *Parsifal*, on January 13, 1882. The very next day, he received the increasingly popular French impressionist, Auguste Renoir (1841–1919), who was also visiting Italy. Renoir was a Wagnerite, though perhaps less than an ardent one. While in Naples, he apparently misplaced a number of letters of introduction to Wagner, written by friends in Paris. Nevertheless, Renoir decided to present himself at the Hotel des Palmes, and there, through the efforts of a kind-hearted Russian painter in Wagner's retinue, the young French artist was introduced to the master.

That day Renoir talked with Wagner for three-quarters of an hour about every imaginable subject: the loss of Renoir's letters of introduction, the controversy stirred by the Paris premier of *Tannhäuser*, Wagner's anti-Semitism. Renoir himself commented on that initial meeting, "We spoke of impressionism in music. What a lot of rubbish I must have talked! Towards the end I was burning with embarrassment, I felt quite giddy and red as a turkey cock. In short, once a shy man gets started he goes too far" (Barth, *Wagner*, 240). At the end of that audience, Wagner granted Renoir time before lunch the next day (in all, thirty-five minutes) to paint his portrait. Surprisingly, Renoir found that amount of time too long, for, toward the end, Wagner lost his good humor and grew stiff, affecting the outcome of the portrait.

The painting found here is the finished version of Renoir's oil sketch, done at noon on January 15, 1882. We know that Renoir found Wagner handsome, even though the completed portrait masks the composer's etched features, his prominent jaw and aquiline nose. In part, of course, this was the result of the brief sitting Renoir was granted, which allowed him to paint no more than a bust pose, with no accompanying furnishings or attributes. In part, too, the absence of strong linear features was a product of Renoir's impressionist technique.

To be sure, one would not mistake the Wagner of this portrait, even though the contours and most of the distinguishing features of his face have been washed out by light. His hair and distinctive sideburns are brushed in loosely. Traces of gold, blue, and purple can be seen in his light-drenched features. The real color interest in the portrait appears in the background, where Wagner's face is set off by a rich, if abstract, field of impressionist hues.

Renoir himself recorded Wagner's reaction to the sketch: "I look like a Protestant minister" (Barth, *Wagner*, 241). The artist himself concurred. The simple background, stiff pose, neck piece, and unflinching formality of the painting must have seemed to Wagner all too similar to the straightforward portraits of clergymen painted by his fellow countrymen.

This portrait was done on Renoir's first trip to Italy. Growing prosperity encouraged him to visit Italy in October 1881. When he first arrived, he stayed briefly in Venice, then in Padua and Florence. In Rome he saw Raphael's frescoes in the Villa Farnesina. Before calling on Wagner at the Hotel des Palmes, Renoir studied the great wall paintings from Pompeii in the Naples Museum. Both sets of paintings impressed him with their classical simplicity and monumentality. In fact, this trip to Italy in part reflected Renoir's growing distrust of the fleeting effects that characterized impressionist painting. Especially in Raphael's frescoes, Renoir found the sense of structure, the clarity of form, and security of line he had been searching for. Evidence of this influence can be seen especially in his work of the mid-1880s.

After he painted this portrait, Renoir seems to have gradually changed his opinion of Wagner. From the 1860s, Renoir had been fond of Wagner's music, if only because of the displeasure it provoked among the French. He had been introduced to it by his fellow impressionist, Frédéric Bazille, and was at least familiar in passing with Wagner's major operas. During his youthful enthusiasm for work of the German composer, Renoir made two drawings of him based on a photograph taken in 1867. There are also two later versions of the maestro by Renoir. A third drawing and another oil of Wagner derive from the portrait represented here.

According to the painter's son, Jean Renoir, his father actually "exchanged insults and came to blows with some of those who could not tolerate the German composer" (Renoir, 188). As a result of a performance of *Die Walküre* at Bayreuth, however, Renoir's enthusiasm for Wagner waned. The influential gallery owner and personal friend of the painter, Ambrose Vollard, records Renoir saying of *Walküre:*

> The screams of the Walkyries are all right for a short time, but when they last six hours on end, you go mad. I decidedly prefer Italian music; it is less pedantic than the German. Even Beethoven has sometimes a professional side that makes my flesh creep. But there is nothing that can touch a little air by Couperin or Grétry—any of the old French music, in fact. There's fine drawing for you. (Vollard, 106–107)

Richard Wagner *by Auguste Renoir (1882), oil on canvas, 53 × 46 cm, Musée du Louvre, Paris*

Charles Gounod

"If you like, I will get you back to Rome with the Grand Prix for Paintings" (Gounod, 68). The great painter and author of our drawing, Jean-Auguste-Dominique Ingres (1780–1867), addressed these words to Charles Gounod (1818–1893). The remark was made during Gounod's first year in Rome, 1840–41, when the future composer was studying music at the French Academy at the Villa Medici. At the time, Ingres, the painter, was the director of this august institution. Ingres had known Gounod's father, François, also a painter, largely because the latter had come in second for the Prix de Rome in 1783. Eventually, the elder Gounod studied in Rome under the auspicies of the French Academy, beginning in 1787.

Charles Gounod was also a skilled draftsman. On seeing a copy Charles made of an image of St. Catherine (from the Early Christian Basilica of S. Clemente in Rome), Ingres asked him for some tracings of original prints. It was on the completion of this task that Ingres offered, partially in jest, to see that Gounod returned to the Villa Medici, this time with a Prix de Rome for painting.

Ingres was a principal figure in the neoclassic tradition in French painting during the first half of the nineteenth century. He also had a great appreciation for music (see p. 60). Certainly it was the neoclassicist in Ingres that drew him to the operas of Christoph Willibald Gluck (see p. 44), "Whose noble style, with its touch of pathos, stamped him [Ingres] in his mind as something of the ancient Greek, a worthy scion of Aeschylus, of Sophocles, or Euripides" (Gounod, 61). These feelings are conveyed to us by Gounod in his *Autobiographical Reminiscences,* from which we also learn that Ingres was "music mad." In addition to the music of Gluck, he admired that of Haydn, Beethoven, and Mozart. Ingres' greatest sympathy was for German music, but the artist was also fond of Rossini and Cherubini. Gounod managed to persuade the director of the French Academy of the appeal of Lully's music.

Music indeed inspired their friendship. Just before Ingres left his post in Rome in 1841, he presented the young Gounod with the sketch of the composer (shown here). In the fashion of Vigée-Lebrun's *Paisiello,* Gounod is seated at the piano looking wistfully over his shoulder as he plays. The score that rests on the piano is, quite appropriately, Mozart's *Don Giovanni.* The composer himself tells us that this was Ingres' favorite opera, one to which Gounod also knew the score. Though he admits to being an unaccomplished pianist, he was often requested to play selections from it for Ingres' enjoyment while the two of them were at the Villa Medici. The inscription in the lower right-hand corner reads: "*Ingres à son jeune ami, M. Gounod, Rome 1841.*"

Ingres, a master draftsman, managed to capture the piano and Gounod's coat in a few carefully articulated strokes. The composer's face, however, retains a soft, innocent charm. Indeed, Gounod was no more than a student then, though one of great promise. His first performed opera, *Sappho,* was ten years away. Its Greek subject reflected Ingres' (and the Academy's) pronounced interest in classical themes. Contemporary critics also found the influence of Ingres' beloved Gluck in the score.

Gounod amply and rather fondly acknowledged some of the general classical notions he had imbibed from Ingres, notions that would continue into the composer's mature years:

Monsieur Ingres was a true apostle of the beautiful.... He shed as much light on a musician's as on a painted work, ushering us all into the presence of the universal sources of the highest truths. By showing me the real nature of true art, he taught me more about my own than any number of merely technical masters could have done. (Gounod, 93)

Charles Gounod was a musician with obvious artistic skills; Ingres was a painter with musical interests and abilities. This collaboration, in the halls of the Villa Medici, obviously enriched both men. Gounod helped and entertained Ingres, who, in turn, gave the young composer a rich set of classical ideals that aided in the development of his own musical style.

Charles Gounod by Jean-Auguste-Dominique Ingres (1841), graphite on paper, 29.9 × 23.3 cm, The Art Institute of Chicago

Clara Schumann

a remarkable first sitting, nothing but being "on view" without canvas or palette—it was very funny. He wanted to study my face before beginning. He thinks he will want only one day for the picture, either it will succeed at once or not at all.

This is Clara Schumann's (1819–1896) own assessment of the method and speed with which Franz von Lenbach characteristically worked (Chissel, 180–181). The resultant portrait reveals a warm, generous spirit, one without pretense, musical or otherwise. Schumann's sympathetic mouth and large eyes convey some of the melancholy felt by the composer. At the time the portrait was painted, she had suffered the mental decline and death of her husband, then the subsequent death of two of her children. The loose treatment of her hair and upper torso are signal qualities of Lenbach's approach to painting in the late 1870s.

Franz von Lenbach (1836–1906) painted his portrait of Clara Schumann in 1878, twenty-five years after her last great period of compositional activity. In 1853, she wrote her Variations on a Theme of Robert Schumann, Op. 20; Three Romances for Piano, Op. 21; Three Romances for Piano and Violin, Op. 22; and Six Songs, Op. 23. It was in the fall of the same fated year that Johannes Brahms was first introduced to the Schumann family, and that J.-J.-B. Laurens drew his sensitive portraits of Brahms (see p. 99) and Robert Schumann (see p. 85).

During her lifetime, Clara Schumann was best known as a performer, a concert pianist. She garnered great attention as a child prodigy, appearing in the Leipzig Gewandhaus at age nine. For the next ten years she performed extensively in Paris, Leipzig, Dresden, and cities of northern Germany. In 1838, she triumphed in Vienna, where she was named Royal and Imperial Chamber Virtuoso. Clearly one of the nineteenth century's most durable concert artists, she performed more than 1300 programs in a career that spanned sixty years.

By comparison, Clara Schumann's activity as a composer lasted only twenty-three years, in part because she was more comfortable as performer than composer, in part because she was never fully satisfied with her compositions. She began writing music with Four Polonaises in 1828, the year she first appeared in public playing the piano. The majority of her oeuvre comprises piano pieces and songs, though she wrote chamber music and a youthful piano concerto. Her more developed works are characterized by lyrical melodies, lively rhythms, and, toward the end, increased compositional complexity.

Lenbach's portrait of Clara Schumann might not have been painted at all had it not been for the musician's grandchildren, who wanted a fine portrait of their famous grandmother. The artist chosen for the task was Franz von Lenbach, portraitist of the leaders of the new Germany. Among other notables, Lenbach painted Kaiser Wilhelm, King Ludwig, and Bismarck. He was equally at home with his peers, treating the painters Arnold Böcklin, Moritz von Schwind, and the architect Gottfried Semper. A gifted amateur musician himself (see p. 108), Lenbach also created portraits of Hans von Bülow, Franz Liszt, Richard Wagner, and his favorite composer, Johann Strauss. His was not a romantic view of the personalities of the new nation. Rather Lenbach concentrated on portraying his sitters with a deft psychological penetration that in many ways offers a striking visualization of the *Realpolitik* that motivated so many of the statesmen he painted.

Lenbach's rise to the position of "Painter of the German Reich" was not an easy one. One of seventeen children, he first trained in his father's profession of stonemason. His talents became apparent when he enrolled in the Polytechnic Institute of Augsburg. From inauspicious origins, Lenbach made his way to Munich where he painted portraits and scenes of Bavarian peasant life. There in 1857 he received recognition for a painting he submitted to the Kunstverein. The following year he won a state stipend and traveled to Rome, then briefly to France. On these and subsequent travels through Europe, he assimilated the techniques of the Dutch masters of the seventeenth century, which he would adopt with uncanny technical skill in his portraits of the composers Edvard Grieg (see p. 108) and Clara Schumann.

Clara Schumann by Franz von Lenbach, 1878, watercolor and chalk on cardboard, 54 × 41 cm, Robert Schumann-Haus, Zwickau, Germany

Anton Bruckner

The career of Anton Bruckner (1824–1896) was characterized by great persistence that helped him rise from humble, rural beginnings to a position of eminence in his native Austria and much of Europe. Widespread international recognition was slow in coming, but his symphonies in particular were widely performed. By 1887 his third and seventh symphonies had been heard in Austria, Germany, Holland, England; also in New York, Boston, and Chicago (Schönzeler).

Throughout his career, Bruckner was eager to prove himself to those in positions of authority. He often requested official statements—testimonials, recommendations—attesting to his musical and personal qualifications, sometimes simply for the record, at other times when he wished to be considered for a specific position, such as organist at St. Florian Abbey.

In time the hoped-for recognition came, and various honors were bestowed on him, to the composer's profound satisfaction. The Order of Emperor Franz Josef, awarded in 1886, was among these, but what Bruckner craved more than any other distinction was an academic rank and title. This may seem surprising to us, but in Austria, even today, titles awarded by the state, including honorary degrees, continue to be viewed as supreme marks of achievement. In Bruckner's case there were special reasons. Manfred Wagner relates in detail Bruckner's attempts to obtain an academic appointment at the University of Vienna, to teach harmony, counterpoint, and composition. Predictably there was much resistance since these subjects customarily were taught at conservatories. One of Bruckner's objectives was to obtain civil-servant status, leading to a regular salary and pension. All he was able to obtain was an appointment as lecturer, at first without pay! An honorary doctorate then seemed to be the most desirable alternative—desired, also, because Brahms had been the recipient of a degree *honoris causa*.

Friends supported Bruckner's petition; it was submitted to the emperor who approved it on September 29, 1891. At this time, these friends and others considered it fitting that a portrait of the composer should be created by a major artist. The sculptor Viktor Tilgner (1844–1896) had that reputation, at least in the Austria of his time. The period of sweeping architectural changes in Vienna, the Ringstrasse era, offered many opportunities to Tilgner, whose statues of

famous Austrians met with official and popular approval. He created busts of the emperor, empress, and Crown Prince Rudolf; his Mozart monument stands in the Burggarten (imperial palace gardens). Other statues by Tilgner were placed in the palace itself, the Burgtheater, and various museums. Tilgner also created busts of Johann Strauss, Liszt, and Brahms, along with a bust of Bellini for the Court Opera, one of the many new public buildings along the Ringstrasse. In 1888 Tilgner became an honorary member of the Academy of Fine Arts in Vienna. In all, he seemed to be the right person for a Bruckner statue.

The honorary degree of Doctor of Philosophy was conferred on Bruckner on November 7, 1891. At the official ceremony he was moved beyond words, barely managing to say: "I cannot thank you as I should like to. If only an organ were here; then I would be able to tell you how I feel" (Novak, 242–243).

Before this, the composer frequently had refused to sit for a portrait, claiming lack of time as the reason. But at this moment his satisfaction and elation were immense, and his friends were quick to recognize the opportune moment. Immediately after the ceremony they took him to Tilgner's studio for the first of several sittings. Tilgner was known to work rapidly, which no doubt pleased the impatient composer.

While there are many portraits and drawings of Bruckner, and countless photographs, Tilgner's work generally is considered the best. It remained in Bruckner's apartment; after his death it was acquired by the Museum of the City of Vienna. It served as the model for Bruckner monuments in the Austrian town of Steyr (1898) and in Vienna (1899).

To judge by some photographs of the same period (such as one showing Bruckner wearing the Order of Franz Josef), Tilgner captured well the composer's features and facial expression. Beyond that, his appearance, including the casual, somewhat rustic and ill-fitting attire, express what we know about the musician's simplicity and lack of pretense in all matters of daily life.

Having finally received the official recognition he so desired, Bruckner lived in virtual seclusion during the last two years of his life. His passing was front-page news in the Viennese press and occasioned close to eighty obituaries and other articles, some describing the funeral at St. Florian in minute detail. Such was the great esteem in which Bruckner was held by many segments of Austrian society, from the imperial family and university faculty and students, to the simple folk of his country origin.

Anton Bruckner *by Viktor Tilgner
(1891), bronzed plaster of Paris, 85 cm,
Museen der Stadt Wien, Vienna*

Johannes Brahms

Johannes Brahms (1833–1897) was only twenty when portrayed by J.-J.-B. Laurens (1801–1896), who was himself both a talented musician and draftsman (see p. 84). This sensitive drawing also bears the abbreviated autograph of the young Brahms's Scherzo in E-flat Minor at the bottom. Laurens executed the sketch at Robert Schumann's request during October of 1853, a month which found both Brahms and Laurens visiting Robert and Clara Schumann in Düsseldorf.

Just prior to the time the portrait was drawn, Brahms had been touring the Rhine. At the insistence of the King of Hanover's concertmaster, Joseph Joachim, and the conductor J. W. von Wasielewski, he called on Robert Schumann. Initially reluctant to make such a visit because Schumann had returned some of Brahms's manuscripts unopened, the younger composer decided to travel to Düsseldorf only after studying pieces by Schumann in detail.

At the time Robert Schumann was suffering some of the more advanced symptoms of mental illness—melancholy, insomnia, nervous disorders. These made his duties in Düsseldorf, where he served as municipal director, especially difficult. Schumann was also preparing for a concert tour of Holland and considering a move to Vienna. In the midst of this hectic, troubled period, Brahms managed to secure his host's attention by playing his own early piano pieces with wide-ranging expressive power. In the days that followed in Düsseldorf, Schumann became a devoted friend and admirer of Brahms, who in turn appreciated the warmth and friendly surroundings he found in the Schumann household.

Schumann was, in fact, so taken by the prodigy that he wrote a short, laudatory article on Brahms which appeared in the Leipzig *Neue Zeitschrift für Musik* at the end of October 1853.

The article stimulated even greater interest in the work of the young virtuoso. When Brahms left Düsseldorf he traveled first to Hanover, then to Leipzig. Schumann had written the publishers Breitkopf & Härtel in Leipzig before Brahms's arrival. Thus, for the second time in a month, Schumann had helped his protege, this time in publishing his first compositions: two piano sonatas, six songs (Op. 3), and the scherzo. Laurens probably wrote out the introduction to this last piece at the bottom of his portrait of Brahms because that composition was so admired by Schumann.

It was during those eventful weeks in October 1853 that Laurens created his drawings of both Schumann and Brahms. Apparently Schumann wanted something with which to remember Brahms, and so had Laurens draw the younger man's features. During Schumann's confinement in the mental hospital in Endenich, he asked for the sketch of Brahms so that he might view it daily. The drawing thus became a sentimental remembrance of the meeting between the two composers.

From photographs of Brahms taken about the time of the sketch, it is evident that Laurens created an exceptionally lifelike portrait. The visiting French musician-artist captured Brahms's delicate, developing features, at the same time bestowing an eternal youthfulness on his subject. This was perhaps best summarized by Schumann's daughter, Maria, who recalled opening the door for Brahms when he first appeared at the Schumann household to find herself in the presence of "a very young man, handsome as a picture, with long blond hair" (MacDonald, 15).

The strength of the profile pose, with the subject looking down, conveys precisely those same qualities which led Schumann to call Brahms the "young eagle." Though a self-trained artist, Laurens had a unique talent, for he succeeded in capturing not only Brahms's appearance, but the air of self-confidence and slight aloofness Brahms possessed as a young man.

Johannes Brahms *by Jean-Joseph-Bonaventure Laurens (1853), pencil, 30 × 25 cm, Bibliothèque Inguimbertine, Carpentras, France*

Modest Mussorgski

The term "nationalism" is generally used for the music of composers like Grieg, Sibelius, and Rimsky-Korsakov, whose portraits are featured in this book. Yet the nationalist aims of both artist *and* composer are nowhere better exemplified than in Ilya Repin's portrait of Modest Mussorgski (1835–1881).

While still a student at the Academy, Repin (1844–1930) met Vladimir Stasov, one of the country's most influential art critics. Stasov would prove to be important in the creation of the *Mussorgski* for two reasons. The critic turned away from western European ideas of art in the late 1850s and first began to champion overtly Russian themes in 1862. It was also Stasov who coined the term *kuchka*, the "Mighty Five," to apply to the group of younger musicians that had formed around Mikhail Glinka: Balakirev, Borodin, Cui, Rimsky-Korsakov, and Modest Mussorgski. Repin met the five at Stasov's, where the group gathered for comradeship and discussion, and to hear each other's recent compositions. Many of these pieces were based on Russian motifs and ideas, an approach that was encouraged, of course, by Stasov.

Repin, however, did not get the chance to paint the portrait in the Tretyakov until the very end of Mussorgski's tragic life. At the time, the composer, an alcoholic, was hospitalized, largely because of the epileptic seizures he suffered. Although the score was disorganized, his *Khovanshchina*, on which he had been working since 1872, then lay almost complete. He had also embarked on a new comic opera, *The Fair at Sorochintsy*. For the last year of his life, however, Mussorgski composed nothing original, though he did arrange several folk songs.

A month before Mussorgski's death, members of the Five secured a bed for their fellow composer in a military hospital in St. Petersburg. Through Stasov, Repin learned of Mussorgski's condition. The portraitist had wanted to paint the composer of the great *Boris Godunov* for ten years and went almost immediately to his bedside. Mussorgski, whose condition had temporarily improved, was delighted to see the painter again. Evidently, the four days that Repin spent on this masterpiece of characterization were happy ones for both artists. Mussorgski got out of bed and posed in an armchair, while Repin, who had no easel in the hospital, worked on a tabletop. The painting was finished on March 5; Mussorgski died eleven days later.

To be certain, Repin captured something of Mussorgski's condition during those last days— the rheumy eyes, flushed features, and unkempt hair and beard. This honest treatment of Mussorgski's alcoholism predictably drew critical protest when the painting was first displayed. Yet the composer's warmth, his honest affections, and above all his spirit come through. Repin knew *Boris Godunov* well, and it is difficult not to see at least a hint of the troubled usurper to the Russian throne in Mussorgski's features here. The colorful regional clothing worn by the composer is certainly not hospital issue. Likewise, the resonant, dark palette adopted by Repin for the portrait conveys a recognizably Russian flavor, which was, after all, a principal aesthetic goal linking the work of both artists.

The painting now resides in the collection of the Tretyakov Gallery. When the great collector Pavel Tretyakov tried to purchase the *Mussorgski* for what was to become the national collection, Repin returned his money. The artist claimed to have received payment enough in the form of the good humor and friendship he had experienced during those four days he had spent painting the composer.

Ilya Repin was a leading member of the *Peredvizhniki*, the Society of Traveling Exhibitions. This group, primarily of younger artists, was drawn together in rebellion against many of the aesthetic aims of the Academy of Art in St. Petersburg, where Repin had studied and achieved considerable recognition.

Drawn to music since his student years, Ilya Repin grew particularly interested in Mussorgski from an early date, before the composer's work was generally recognized. Fan and Stephen Parker have translated a letter from Repin to Vladimir Stasov, which reveals Mussorgski's appeal to the great Russian portraitist:

> At present I too would have liked so much to listen to Russian music, especially the music of Moussorgsky, the essence of Russian music (I dare to think). In my memory so frequently arises [sic] his melodies, as of many [Russian composers]. I recall your marvelous, poetic evenings which we spent together in the company of many.... Could such a marvelous period of life, so full of meaning, national, original, in the circle of friends, be repeated? (Parker, 30)

Modest Mussorgski *by Ilya Repin (1881), oil on canvas, 69 × 57 cm, Russian Museum, Leningrad*

Piotr Ilyich Tchaikovsky

Never have I been so worn out by conducting as in Odessa, for I had to conduct five concerts. . . . If some day I could only receive in our two capitals one-tenth of the honors showered on me in Odessa! But that is impossible, and besides, I don't really need it. What I need is to believe in myself again, for my faith in myself is terribly shattered, and it seems to me that my role has ended.

TCHAIKOVSKY IN A LETTER TO HIS BROTHER MODEST, FEBRUARY 9, 1893, AT THE TIME THIS PORTRAIT WAS PAINTED

For some 100 years now the music of Piotr Ilyich Tchaikovsky (1840–1893) has held a place of distinction, enjoying international popularity. His orchestral works in particular—symphonies, concertos, concert overtures, ballet music—continue to have a firm place in the standard repertory throughout the Western world and beyond, wherever classical music is heard. His life story, too, has fascinated the public, then and today; not surprisingly it has been romanticized and fictionalized, giving rise to an extensive literature. The many problems he struggled with in his personal life did not prevent his tremendous success as a composer, though there were setbacks, periods of self-doubt, and other obstacles. During his lifetime, much of his music was performed throughout Europe and beyond. His first piano concerto received its world premiere in Boston in 1875; the composer himself was celebrated during an American tour in 1891.

Frequent travels continued. Early in 1893 he went to Switzerland, then to Brussels, conducting programs that included some of his own works. Soon he returned to Russia to fulfil engagements in Odessa. The schedule was grueling, leading to the feelings of frustration and depression vented in the letter quoted above (Weinstock, 353).

In spite of this, Tchaikovsky immediately began composing the Sixth Symphony, and work, surprisingly, went well. "You cannot imagine what happiness I experience at the conviction that my time is not yet over," he wrote to his brother-in-law (Weinstock, 354).

It was precisely at this busy time that Nikolay Kuznetsov painted Tchaikovsky's portrait. The artist was born in Odessa in 1850. Soon after he painted Tchaikovsky he became a professor at the St. Petersburg Academy of Art. He was a member of Artel, an artists' cooperative that tried to gain wider recognition for its members by organizing traveling exhibits, a project that continued until after the Revolution. Kuznetsov regularly contributed to the exhibits. Several oil portraits by him found their way into the prestigious Tretyakov Gallery.

The collaboration of these two artists, then, took place during a stressful period in Tchaikovsky's life. The finished portrait must have cheered him somewhat; he was impressed by "its expressiveness and vividness," thought it realistic and "really wonderful." Brother Modest also praised its authenticity and its realism, recognizing his brother's "cold, dark, intense gaze" (Warrack, 204).

The generally very dark tones of the painting convey, at first, a gloomy impression. Certainly the composer's mien is serious and intense, but not unfriendly or angry. His brow is furrowed; he seems to be looking down—at the painter, not the viewer. His right hand rests on an open music score: it is not clearly painted, in contrast to so many musicians' portraits of earlier centuries, in which we can often establish with certainty the exact composition represented. In Kuznetsov's portrait we see

> a deep-thinking, rather care-worn but not humorless white-haired man who might be a well-preserved sixty-five. With Tchaikovsky, not yet fifty-three, the aging process was accelerating to a most alarming degree, as he filled his life more and more with feverish activity. (Garden, 138)

This activity continued through the period of composing the Sixth Symphony, the "Pathétique." It received its first performance on October 28, 1893, in St. Petersburg. Tchaikovsky considered it "the best of my compositions," and the judgment of many listeners since then would confirm this view. Yet its initial reception was merely polite—another source of dejection for the composer.

A little more than a week later Tchaikovsky was dead. The circumstances of his passing—supposedly death from cholera, probably contracted intentionally by drinking unboiled water—have never been established unequivocally. Several factors point to suicide: an earlier attempt, soon after his unsuccessful marriage in 1877; an unpleasant encounter, shortly before his death, with a woman intending to blackmail him because of his relationship with her son. The circumstances of his death, together with aspects of the composer's lifestyle, are discussed in detail by David Brown ("Tchaikovsky" in *The New Grove Dictionary*).

Piotr Ilyich Tchaikovsky by Nikolay Kuznetzov (1893), oil, Russian Museum, Leningrad

Emmanuel Chabrier

In this painting of Emmanuel Chabrier (1841–1894), Édouard Manet (1832–1883) used a slight variation of the portrait type he had earlier reserved for such writers as Zacharie Astruc, Emile Zola, and Stéphane Mallarmé. In these portraits, he had shown his subjects off to one side of the painting, counterbalanced by objects of their trade—books and writing implements on a table beside them. Their faces are either turned aside, or, if they look to the front, their eyes seem to penetrate the viewer.

In our portrait, Chabrier occupies the center of the composition. His torso is inclined informally from the left, while he rests his head on his hand, as if lost in thought. A sheet of music occupies the lower right corner of the painting in much the same way books are found in his portraits of authors. Chabrier gazes beyond the composition with eyes so loosely painted they lose their focus. In places they even fuse with the surrounding sockets. This evanescent technique corresponds nicely with some of the more suggestive chromatic tone painting of the late nineteenth- and early twentieth-century French composers d'Indy, Debussy, Ravel, and Ibert.

For the ten years preceding his death, Édouard Manet was one of Chabrier's closest friends. The two men were neighbors from 1879 to 1884, and Chabrier often attended the Thursday soirees at Manet's studio. In his youth Chabrier himself thought of becoming a painter, and his interest in the medium never flagged. He was an ardent admirer of the impressionists and supported their revolutionary ideas, which in many respects were similar to his own in music. Chabrier began to purchase the work of Claude Monet as early as 1878 when he bought the *La rue Saint Denis*. On the occasion of the fourth independent impressionist exhibition the next year, he purchased at least three more paintings by Monet, with whom Chabrier shared a fondness for visiting the French coast, particularly in Brittany and Normandy.

In 1878 Chabrier wrote his wife from Etretat (a location Monet frequently painted slightly later in his life): "The sea, the beloved sea is still there and you know just how much I love it. . . . Its hugeness makes me think of a thousand different things, as do the sunsets, the sunsets with all those gold and purple tints . . ." (Delage, 19).

When Manet died, Chabrier purchased a number of his paintings too, including his final large salon painting, the well-known *The Bar at the Folies-Bergère*. At the time of his own death,

Chabrier owned seven oils by Manet, six by Monet, three by Renoir, and one by Cézanne. In addition, his collection contained several drawings and prints by the impressionists.

Today concert audiences best know Emmanuel Chabrier for his *España*, composed in 1883. The previous year, Chabrier set out on a six-month tour of the Iberian peninsula, including stops at Burgos, Toledo, Seville, Granada, Malaga, Cordoba, Valencia, and Barcelona. It was this trip that inspired the orchestral rhapsody, *España*, based on the songs of Andalusia. It would be interesting to discover whether Manet played a role in Chabrier's decision to visit Spain. After all, Manet painted Chabrier's portrait in 1881, only a year before the composer's trip.

As early as 1860, Manet had developed his own interest in Spanish subjects, the chief influence on his art throughout the decade. Looking to painters as divergent as Velázquez and Goya, Manet produced such important subjects as the *Spanish Singer* (1860), *The Old Musician* (1862), and *Mlle. V. in the Costume of an Espada* (1864) in an older Spanish style.

Based on the stark contrasts favored by Spanish painters, Manet evolved a style that featured brilliantly lighted, large-scale figures set against dark backgrounds. In defiance of classical artistic practice, his loose, bold manner of painting shocked members of the French Academy. Along with Gustav Courbet, Manet was one the most important realist painters who worked in Paris in the 1860s. His love for scenes of contemporary, bourgeois life framed a set of subjects on which the impressionists would draw again and again. Inspired by Manet, Edgar Degas, for instance, would paint similar haunts—stage, concert hall, race track.

The warmth and sympathy found in Manet's portrait are qualities which Chabrier is said to have possessed in life. These are similar to the emotions which Chabrier often managed to fix, in a more fleeting manner, in the sonority, colors, and mood of his music. Manet must have sensed this uncanny ability in the composer when he painted Chabrier with the understanding and psychological insight only a close friend could bring to the portrait of a fellow artist.

Emmanuel Chabrier *by Édouard Manet (1881), oil on canvas, 65 × 53.5 cm, The Fogg Art Museum, Cambridge, MA*

Arthur Sullivan

Perhaps nowhere in this present volume are the talents of composer and artist so evenly matched as those of the witty, gifted Arthur Sullivan (1842–1900) and the equally gifted, prolific John Everett Millais (1829–1896). Both were clearly among the most popular British artists working in their respective mediums at the end of the nineteenth century. Sullivan himself was knighted and at least ten of his comic operas are regularly produced today, a fate that has escaped every other master of the genre, with perhaps the exception of Rossini (see p. 70). Millais, on the other hand, was a founder and member of the Pre-Raphaelite Brotherhood, and later president of the Royal Academy.

In the late 1860s, composer and painter met at London's famous Garrick Club. There both men enjoyed socializing, dining, gambling; more importantly they developed an interest in each other that would last until Millais's death in 1896. Shortly after they met, they collaborated on a song cycle, *The Window,* or *The Songs of the Wrens,* with Alfred Tennyson writing the lyrics, Millais providing illustrations to each song. Tennyson experienced qualms about the project and Millais eventually used most of the drawings he did for the project to other ends.

Sullivan recalled of the collaboration (to Millais's son, John Guille Millais, for the latter's tribute to his father, *The Life and Letters of Sir John Everett Millais*):

> It had long been my desire and ambition to do a work which should combine the three sister Arts, poetry, painting and music.... The first and only [illustration] done I remember well. It was a lovely drawing of a girl at a window, birds flying around and vine and eglantine trailing about it. (Millais, 421)

According to the younger Millais, this drawing was sold and used apparently for two purposes: for the frontispiece for Henry Leslie's "Little Songs" and as an illustration in *Cassell's Family Magazine.*

The close friends, Sullivan and Millais, collaborated again on a later project, one in which Sullivan would himself be the subject—the portrait illustrated here. Sullivan was between work on *Ruddigore* and the more successful *Yeomen of the Guard* when he was painted by Millais in early 1888. The artist chose to show his friend in a manner that reflected his financial and social success. He painted Sir Arthur Sullivan, the apparently nonchalant *bon vivant,* in frock coat and tie. The composer's hands rest on the arm of the chair, which subtly separates him from the viewer. His gaze slides off on an angle, carefully directed to avoid anyone looking at him. Millais rendered Sullivan's face with almost photographic detail, choosing to subordinate the rest of the body and the background with looser brushwork. Sullivan recorded in his diary that Millais's portrait of him presented a memorable likeness.

One critic, who evidently saw the painting on private display just before it was completed, did not respond as favorably. He found the artist's vision and psychological penetration remarkable, but questioned the work's lack of finish. Still the Millais is unique, for it gives us an image of the way Sullivan presented himself in fashionable British society—a reserved, accomplished gentleman, not the light-hearted composer of the jaunty melodies that accompanied such playful W. S. Gilbert lyrics as "I Am the Very Model of a Modern Major General" or "If You Want to Know Who We Are."

Sir Arthur Sullivan by John Everett Millais (1888), oil on canvas, 115.6 × 87 cm, National Portrait Gallery, London

Edvard Grieg

Edvard Grieg (1843–1907) had a long association with Germany. He attended the conservatory in Leipzig for four years from 1858 to 1862. There he heard Clara Schumann perform at the piano. Lenbach would paint her portrait in 1878 (see p. 94) and Grieg's some twelve years later. Invitations to conduct and play the piano also brought the Norwegian composer to Germany frequently. The native land of Richard Wagner held one last attraction: Bayreuth. Grieg attended the first installment of the *Ring* there in 1876, and also heard *Parsifal* in 1883.

The music of Wagner also attracted Franz von Lenbach (1836–1906), "Painter of the German Reich," who similarly traveled as a pilgrim to Bayreuth. There he, like Grieg, heard *Parsifal,* which he praised. He also attended the first performance of *Die Meistersinger* given at Bayreuth. Soon, however, Lenbach distanced himself from Wagner, in part, at least, because he was suspicious of opera. Instead, he favored instrumental music. While Lenbach had little musical training, he apparently had a gift for playing the harmonium (the parlor organ). In the foyer of his studio he installed a piano, on which he would improvise on works by Bach and Handel. Boccherini, Haydn, Mozart, and Edvard Grieg also numbered among his favorite composers.

After completing his studies at the Leipzig Conservatory, the Norwegian-born Grieg settled in Copenhagen, where he first came into contact with exponents of Norwegian nationalism in language, politics, and music. Even though Denmark had ceded mainland Norway to Sweden at the beginning of the century, Norwegian language and cultural life were still dominated by Danish forms and values. As early as Grieg's Op. 6, *Humoresque* (1865), the composer's conversion to distinctive Norwegian rhythms and harmonies can be heard. The following year, Grieg began collecting and writing piano versions of Norwegian folk songs.

After returning to Norway to live in 1866, Grieg wrote his best-known compositions, the Piano Concerto, Op.16 (1868), and his *Peer Gynt Suite*, Op. 46 (1874–75). During this period, he also took prominent roles in establishing national musical organizations, the Norwegian Academy of Music and the Christiania Musikforening. Much of his uncommitted time was devoted to composing vocal music, based either on Norwegian folk songs, or on reminiscences of Norwegian country life. By the time Lenbach painted this portrait, Grieg had grown accustomed to devoting his spring and summer vacations to composition at his house in Troldhaugen. He would spend the fall and winter in concert appearances throughout England, France, Germany, and Holland.

Grieg may have sat for this portrait sometime between 1883 (when he visited Bayreuth) and 1890 at the latest. The date 1887 suggests itself. In that year, Grieg completed and published his Third Sonata for Violin and Piano in C minor, Op. 45. The piece was inspired by the Italian violinist, Teresina Tua, but dedicated to Lenbach.

Grieg need not have actually posed for the artist. A number of photographs of the composer were available for Lenbach to work from, though none was copied directly for this portrait. The influence of the old masters can be found, especially in Lenbach's brushwork. The treatment of the body, which fades almost completely into the background, is especially reminiscent of portraits by Rembrandt. In later life, Lenbach greatly admired the work of Diego Velázquez. The Spanish painter's inspiration can be seen in the monochromatic palette, and especially in the deft, filmy treatment of the sitter's facial features. The final product, however, is unmistakably by Lenbach. The subtle, shifting coloration of the face and flowing hair and the tightly painted eyes are all characteristic devices which Lenbach used to animate his sitters. In these qualities one can find something of the spirit of the composer who brought the puckish, irrepressible *Peer Gynt* to life.

At the time this portrait was painted both artists had achieved fame for themselves in their respective artistic professions—Grieg throughout the Western world, Lenbach in Germany. So great were the recognition and subsequent financial success accorded the German portraitist that he initiated construction on a great, neobaroque villa for himself in the suburbs of Munich in the same year Grieg completed the violin sonata dedicated to him. The Lenbachhaus, in whose collection the Lenbach *Grieg* is found, is now open to the public and features a large portion of the portrait record of nineteenth-century Germany painted by the mansion's creator.

Edvard Grieg by Franz von Lenbach (c. 1890), oil and pencil on cardboard, 77.5 × 59 cm, Städtische Galerie im Lenbachhaus, Munich

Nicolay Rimsky-Korsakov

When Valentin Serov (1865–1911) portrayed Nicolay Rimsky-Korsakov (1844–1908) at age fifty-four, the composer was enjoying a fruitful period in his career. The year 1898 found the great orchestral colorist preoccupied with opera, or rather with no fewer than four operas. *Sadko,* the mythic fairy tale about which Rimsky-Korsakov had been thinking for years, was triumphantly ending its inaugural run at the Solodovnikov Theater in Moscow. At the same time, the composer was also experiencing problems with the production of his one-act opera, *Mozart and Salieri,* which he had finished writing the previous year. In addition, he had revised *The Maid of Pskov* for production that year, and had also completed virtually the whole of *The Czar's Bride.*

It seems little wonder then that Serov chose to paint the composer in his study, manuscripts piled high on his desk and on the cabinet in the background. The subject might easily be mistaken for a scholar, for the manuscript pages lack any indication of staff lines or musical notation. Indeed, Rimsky-Korsakov seems fully preoccupied with the serious task at hand, as well he might, given the number of projects on which he was engaged at the time.

So stern is the sitter's demeanor, it seems there was no time for mirth while he sat for his portrait. We know, however, that on at least one occasion the opposite was the case. In his *Reminiscences of Rimsky-Korsakov,* the composer's close friend V. V. Yastrebtsev informs us:

> With mock seriousness, Rimsky-Korsakov tried to convince Serov that he wanted terribly to look younger in the portrait and most important of all, he would like his frock coat and cravat to be slightly darker blue. This occasioned much laughter. (p. 204)

The style of the portrait is also noteworthy. Painted at the turn of the century, it reveals just how transitional a figure Serov was in Russian painting. The spirit of the work is generally realist in its sedate color scheme and in the studious pose of its sitter. On the other hand, Serov's restrained, Russian translation of impressionist ideas is revealed in the light into which the sitter stares and the bravura treat-ment of virtually all the objects in the room. Indeed, the painter's deft, creamy treatment of every surface in the composition parallels the orchestral lushness and chromaticism of Rimsky-Korsakov's most exotic scores.

Today, the work of Valentin Serov is too little known in the West. This fact owes not so much to his lack of talent or intellectual ability as to the era in which he painted. Serov was literally an artist astride two centuries. He was named an academician in the year he painted Rimsky-Korsakov's portrait, yet renounced that title in 1905 after witnessing events in the brutal government suppression of uprisings of that year.

He sympathized initially with the aims of the *Peredvizhniki,* a more conservative group of naturalistic painters who employed populist themes. Later Serov allied himself with *Mir iskusstva,* World of Art, a loose movement of Russian moderns who were responsible for the rapid assimilation of ideas from late nineteenth-century France into Russian artistic life.

Serov had the ideal credentials as a portraitist of musicians. He had studied extensively with Ilya Repin, who painted portraits of both Mussorgski (p. 100) and Glinka (p. 78). In addition, his mother was the talented pianist, Valentina Bergmann, who also composed operas. His father, Alexander Nikolayevich, was the noted Wagnerian composer whose operas *Judith* (1863) and *Rogenda* (1865) were immensely popular in the Russia of their day.

After studying with Repin, Alexander Nikolayevich's son, Valentin, set out on a more independent course than his master. He visited the great universal exhibition in Paris in 1889, gaining there firsthand knowledge of modern French artists, especially Bastien-Lepage and Degas.

While Serov painted scenes of peasant life, historical subjects, and landscapes, he was most successful as a painter of portraits. He represented Czar Nicholas II, members of the imperial family, and a host of musicians: Alexander Glazunov, Wanda Landowska, and the singers Chaliapin, Masini, and Tamagno. Other leading Russian artists sat for Serov, among them the writers Gorky and Pushkin, and the impresario Diaghilev. Growing up in a household of musicians gave the young painter a feeling of ease in the company of artists. His talent and skill at composition accomplished the rest.

Nicolay Rimsky-Korsakov *by Valentin Serov (1898),*
oil on canvas, 94 × 111 cm, Tretyakov Gallery, Moscow

Gabriel Fauré

Like all of Sargent's noncommissioned works, this head of Fauré is distinguished by freedom from conventions of portraiture. The raised head and the incisive lines thus formed make a pattern of beauty. . . . The pose is striking, the result of a study the artist made of his model. The position is that of a short man playing the piano, head thrown back, eyes cast down to the keyboard.

CHARLES MERRILL MOUNT

Gabriel Fauré (1845–1924), one of France's outstanding late-romantic composers, came from southern France—the Midi, a region for which he retained a great fondness throughout his long life. When he was still a boy he was sent to Paris to attend the École Niedermeyer, a new training institution for choirmasters and organists. Saint-Saëns, on the piano faculty there, was to have a strong, lasting influence on Fauré, as his teacher and beyond that as a mentor who opened many doors for him.

After several years as an organist in Rennes, Fauré returned to Paris and soon saw military service during the Franco-Prussian War of 1870–1871.

He then assisted Saint-Saëns as organist at the Church of the Madeleine, where Fauré's *Requiem* (first version) was first performed in 1888; he became the official organist at the Madeleine in 1896. By then he also taught at the Conservatoire, becoming its director in 1905. Among his students there, Ravel became his favorite. Fauré's music, his songs in particular, exerted a strong influence on Ravel who dedicated his string quartet to his teacher.

Fauré was now at the height of his career and the recipient of various honors: Commander of the Légion d'Honneur and member of the prestigious Institut de France. Yet he remained a modest person to the end. His state funeral at the Madeleine was an elaborate, moving ceremony; the music included his own *Requiem*.

That John Singer Sargent (1856–1925) completed several portraits of Fauré is largely due to the painter's lifelong devotion to music. Sargent, an American who spent much of his creative life in Europe, became greatly admired and sought after as a portraitist. He was commissioned to paint many celebrities from all walks of life, including presidents Theodore Roosevelt and Woodrow Wilson, the Duke of Marlborough, writers Henry James, Robert Louis Stevenson, and William Butler Yeats, and actor John Barrymore.

Sargent must have been an accomplished pianist, capable of executing challenging accompaniments such as that of Lalo's *Symphonie Espagnole*, which he played for Charles Martin Loeffler, the young American violinist, in 1887. By then Sargent had become acquainted with Fauré's First Violin Sonata (1876), which Loeffler and Sargent enjoyed playing.

Sargent met Fauré in 1889 (probably not for the first time) when Sargent was in Paris, painting and attending the International Exhibition. Our portrait stems from this time.

Even in Paris, Fauré was slow to establish himself as a composer and to make advantageous connections. To make himself known in England he journeyed there several times. Sargent, an admirer of his music and well-connected in English artistic circles and high society, was quite successful in helping Fauré. Maeterlinck's drama *Pelléas and Mélisande* was produced in London in 1898. The star of that production was the actress Mrs. Patrick Campbell. She had met Fauré at the home of Frank Schuster, a wealthy banker, and persuaded Fauré to write incidental music for the play. When he returned to England to conduct the stage production, Fauré, Sargent, and Mrs. Campbell met again at Schuster's country home. Two fine charcoal drawings were done at that time, one of Fauré alone, the other with Mrs. Campbell.

Late in life, in spite of honors and successes, Fauré at times found himself in financial straits. Sargent helped him with a substantial gift of money; he also helped arrange the purchase of several Fauré scores by Harvard University. Fauré in return gave him the manuscript of his Second Piano Quintet, Op. 115 (1921).

Sargent inscribed our painting "A Gabriel Fauré, souvenir affectueux."

Gabriel Fauré by John Singer Sargent (1889), oil on canvas, 54 × 49.5 cm, Conservatoire National Supérieur de Musique, Paris

Gustav Mahler

That gaunt face was a true mirror of its owner's every inner emotion, for which reason it is diversely portrayed by many people, according to the diversity of their relationship with Mahler.
ALFRED ROLLER

Gustav Mahler (1860–1911) was one of the last great representatives of musical romanticism, standing at the threshold of the New Music of the twentieth century. It is perhaps symbolic of this position that Arnold Schoenberg dedicated his major treatise on harmony, published in 1911, to the memory of Mahler.

From beginnings in a small Bohemian village, Mahler's career in time led him to what was then and still is the most prestigious musical position in Austria: the directorship of the Vienna Opera. In 1897, during the reign of Emperor Franz Joseph I, it still was the "Imperial-Royal Court Opera."

The assignment was as stressful as it was prestigious. Mahler was determined to introduce many changes, especially to raise artistic standards. This, in a conservative institution, caused much resentment and foot dragging. Artistic and administrative duties fully occupied Mahler during the opera season, leaving for composition only the precious summer months, when he could get away from the city.

Mahler reaped great artistic successes, not only at home but throughout Europe, and eventually in America. His fiftieth birthday was celebrated with a publication presenting tributes from famous artists in many fields: the dramatists Gerhart Hauptmann and Hugo von Hofmannsthal; the composers Richard Strauss and Max Reger; the conductor Bruno Walter, and many others. It also contained the first reproduction of Rodin's bust of Mahler, with greetings from the artist.

Today's appreciation of Mahler's music essentially goes back to the late 1950s and 1960s. Much of it must be credited to the enthusiasm of Leonard Bernstein who, as conductor of the New York Philharmonic, presented Mahler's music in epoch-making performances. Through broadcasts and recordings they reached a national and international audience, many listeners previously having been unacquainted with Mahler's name, let alone his music.

During his years at the Vienna Opera, Mahler developed an interest in the visual arts; it was stimulated by contacts with a group of artists associated with the Secession. Among the artists whose works were exhibited by the "Secessionists" were Cézanne, Munch—and Rodin.

Viennese members of the group included Gustav Klimt and Alfred Roller. The latter in particular inspired Mahler to an awareness of what the visual arts could do for the stage. A fruitful collaboration developed between Mahler and Roller as a stage designer, beginning with a *Tristan* production in 1903. Best known today probably are Roller's designs for the *Rosenkavalier* production of 1911—sets that were unexcelled and remained in use for over fifty years.

Mahler's ties to the Secession found musical expression when, in 1902, he took an active part in a Max Klinger exhibition which included a Beethoven monument (see pp. 64f.). For this occasion Mahler arranged and conducted an excerpt from Beethoven's Ninth Symphony.

Auguste Rodin (1840–1917) and Mahler met in Paris in 1909, where the latter was staying on his return from New York. According to Mahler's wife, Alma Maria, Carl Moll (1861–1945), one of the early members of the Secession and Alma's stepfather, had commissioned Rodin to do a bronze bust of Mahler. Alma relates that "Rodin fell in love with his model, and he was quite desolate when we wanted to leave; he wanted to continue working on Mahler." He was fascinated with Mahler's head and sculpted (or possibly had his assistant sculpt) another one, in marble, for himself. Rodin, according to Alma, saw the composer's head as incorporating features of King Frederick the Great, Benjamin Franklin, and Mozart. Strangely enough, the marble bust, in the Musée Rodin in Paris, is labelled "Mozart," though the resemblance to Rodin's bronze bust of Mahler is evident. (According to Gartenberg, it was so labelled by the curator of the Rodin Museum. The matter is also discussed by Grunfeld in his Rodin biography.) The sculptor's fondness for Mozart is well known; it also seems that Rodin was quite casual about renaming his creations.

Rodin's bronze bust of Mahler is housed, quite appropriately, in the foyer of the Vienna State Opera, where thousands of admirers have seen it before performances and during intermissions. Aside from being an exquisite work of art, it also is a fine likeness of the composer. This is confirmed by a comparison with the many photos of Mahler, assembled for the first time and annotated with love and care by Alfred Roller. Additional photographs are reproduced in Blaukopf's splendid documentary study. Mahler was not tall, but robust and muscular—a great hiker, fond of swimming, rowing, and bicycling. Much of this changed after he was diagnosed as having a congenital heart defect (1907). Roller, who had known Mahler since 1900, points out that observers disagreed on the expressive qualities of Mahler's face: some con-

Gustav Mahler *by*
Auguste Rodin (1909),
bronze, 34 × 24 × 22 cm,
foyer, State Opera House,
Vienna

sidered it handsome, others emphatically did not. His features impressed some as serious, strict, or rigid; others saw someone who was nervous and impatient; others still found that he looked accessible and likeable (K. Blaukopf, 12). What we can conclude from this variety, and from our own examination of the pictorial evidence, is that Mahler was an extremely sensitive artist whose face easily reflected the moods and emotions of a given moment.

Among other Mahler portraits the most significant are a drawing by Fritz Erler and a painting and engraving by Emil Orlik, the latter also a member of the Secession. Among the persons represented in Klimt's Beethoven frieze is a knight whose facial features (intentionally) resemble those of Mahler. Finally there is the composer's death mask, taken by Carl Moll.

Claude Debussy

Yesterday, I went to the Salon d'Automne to see an exhibition by Henry de Groux. . . . It's a wonderful exhibition! . . . A large bronze of Tolstoy marching, as it seems, in the face of Destiny, much finer than Rodin's ingenious mutilations! A portrait of Wagner, looking like an old, cynical magician, guarding his secret. . . . A whole succession of images and shapes which haunt you continuously. I saw de Groux there, hardly changed. Still giving the impression of a talented clown, with all the dreams of the world in his eyes.

It was in a letter to Robert Godet that Claude Debussy himself made this assessment of Henry de Groux's contribution to the 1911 Salon d'Automne (Lesure, 214–215). The Salon, of which de Groux's series of busts of famous artists was such an integral part, was an annual exhibition, usually of more venturesome artists, held each autumn in Paris starting in 1903.

Though Debussy (1862–1918) was far from an art critic, he was at least familiar with the work of Turner and the impressionists. He seems to have known the work of the latter artists less directly than might otherwise be supposed, since the term impressionism is so frequently applied to such works of his as *La Mer, Images,* and *l'Après-midi d'un faune.* There is something about the genuinely pictorial, atmospheric nature of these pieces that lends itself to be regarded as impressionistic. Based on the testimony of his letters, however, Debussy was more familiar with painters who were roughly his contemporaries, the symbolists, than he was with the impressionists. Though Debussy knew and liked the work of Maurice Denis and Odilon Redon, it was the symbolist painter and later sculptor, Henry de Groux, for whom he reserved his greatest praise.

De Groux (1867–1930) was Belgian, the son of a painter. He studied at the Académie des Beaux-Arts in Brussels, then caused something of a scandal in 1890 with the display of his *Christ Insulted* in the Salon des Beaux-Arts in Brussels. Between 1890 and 1897, he exhibited symbolist paintings on religious and historical subjects, images produced in many cases by hallucination. These self-concocted mythologies featured casts as far-flung as Caesar, Christ, Napoleon, Nero, Orestes, Savonarola, and Siegfried. All were painted with a spirited approach to form, and especially, to color. During this period, de Groux also conceived visionary portraits of Baudelaire, Wagner, and Zola.

Before these were realized, however, de Groux's personal pantheon of great artists had to wait for the painter to teach himself the difficult technique of bronze casting. Then he created unusual portraits of Baudelaire, Beethoven, Dante, Tolstoy, and the bust of Claude Debussy illustrated here. When these were displayed at the Salon d'Automne of 1911, they stirred strong, very mixed reactions. Critics easily recognized the influence of Rodin (see pp. 114f.), and also noted that these works were more intense even than the portraits of that renowned French sculptor. De Groux's unrestrained, indeed almost obsessive psychological penetration can be seen in the unusual pose of Debussy, in the rough border of the bust, and in the uneven, exaggerated modeling of the composer's facial features. Deeply moved by the powerful creations of the various artists whose busts he sculpted, de Groux sought to convey his own personal interpretation of his subjects in a style that could almost be termed expressionist.

How did Debussy react to this rendering of himself? His letters reveal that he thought all de Groux's portraits in the Salon d'Automne (his own included) represented an outstanding example of moral courage, primarily because of the sculptor's apparent disregard for officially sanctioned taste.

Perhaps Debussy's opinion reflects more his own musical circumstances at the time than an objective reaction to de Groux's portraits. The composer's last work to premier before the Salon d'Automne of 1911 was his setting of Gabriele d'Annunzio's curious *Martyrdom of St. Sebastian.* Debussy had only two months to work on the music that accompanied the play, which ran five hours. Both the short time he had to prepare his *St. Sebastian* and the length of the performance guaranteed negative critical response. Debussy's biographer, Marcel Dietschy, proclaimed that "with *The Martyrdom of St. Sebastian* began the martyrdom of Claude Debussy" (Lockspeiser, 162). It is small wonder that the composer found it easy to sympathize with de Groux whose show, in which this portrait was first displayed, was regarded by one critic as "an artistic witches' sabbath" (Vollmer, 115).

Claude Debussy *by Henry de Groux (1909), bronze, 80 cm, Bibliothèque et Musée de l'Opéra, Paris*

Frederick Delius

Max Beckmann (1884–1950) created this portrait when Frederick Delius visited Germany to take the cure at Wiesbaden in 1922. For a long time Delius had experienced certain effects of syphilis, which contributed to sporadic irritability, failing eyesight, and pain in his arms and legs. None of this is apparent in Beckmann's portrait, with perhaps one exception—the area of the eyes, one of which is larger, more open than the other. The composer was to go blind in 1925 and had difficulty with his eyesight before then.

Even with this slight anomaly, the portrait is an especially sympathetic one, done in Beckmann's best postwar manner. It reveals firm, straight lines in the face. These capture effectively Delius's features, known from photographs. Slight distortions in the jaw, ears, and length of the nose give the composer a subtle animation, as only Beckmann could. That is not to say the artist lied about what he saw. He just mildly emphasized certain features in keeping with the composer's appearance. Clearly, the artist recognized in his sitter the great humanity for which Delius was known. And, no small tribute to Beckmann's own humanity, he was able to bring out that warmth in this sympathetic portrait.

By the time the English-born Frederick Delius (1862–1934) had reached the age of thirty, he had already traveled extensively in the United States, Germany, and Norway. From 1888 he would make his home in France, settling first at locations in and around Paris, then ultimately moving to Grez-sur-Loing in 1897. It was during his years in Paris that Delius became interested in the visual arts, an interest that would last the rest of his life.

By 1894, the composer was moving in the circle of the great symbolist painter Paul Gauguin, only recently returned from his first stay in Tahiti. A group of other artists, including the designer Alphonse Mucha, the writer August Strindberg, and Delius himself, formed around Gauguin, who held weekly soirees for artists at his quarters on the rue de la Grande Chaumière in Montparnasse. Delius would introduce his new friend, the Norwegian painter and printmaker, Edvard Munch, to the circle shortly after Gauguin left once again for Tahiti in 1895. It was in this same year that Delius began his *Koanga*, whose exotic subject matter and bold orchestral treatment were at least in part a product of Gauguin's influence.

Delius's friendship with Munch would last the rest of the composer's life. Delius would be instrumental in promoting Munch's art in Paris, to the point of arranging exhibitions for him there. Until 1922, the two visited one another, both in France and in Norway.

Also situated on the rue de la Grande Chaumière was the important art school, the Académie Colarossi, next to which Gauguin temporarily lived in 1893. One of the students at the Académie was Jelka Rosen, a young German painter then living with her mother in Paris. She and Delius met in 1896 and married in 1903. An excellent artist who worked in a post-impressionist manner, Jelka also left an important portrait record of the composer. She was a great admirer of Auguste Rodin (see pp. 114f.) and introduced Delius to the French sculptor.

Unlike the powerful influence of Gauguin, or the long friendship with Munch, Delius's acquaintance with Max Beckmann was brief. Apparently, the two knew one another only from the composer's visits to Frankfurt in 1922 and 1923. On the first of these, Delius stopped briefly for a performance of his *Requiem*. At the time, he was in Germany for longer stays at Wiesbaden and Wildbad, both spas which Delius visited in hopes of improving his deteriorating health.

Max Beckmann, himself a highly individualistic German expressionist, settled in Frankfurt-am-Main in 1915. He moved there after suffering a nervous breakdown, the result of a year's wartime service in the medical corps, first in East Prussia, then in Flanders. By his own account, he ended up in Frankfurt because he liked the city and had friends there. In the years before World War I, Beckmann had painted generally large-scale historical and mythological subjects in a rather somber expressionist manner. While he was recovering in Frankfurt, his art changed dramatically. Freely based on religious subjects, his paintings became more angular and crowded. Most tellingly, his forms were usually described with strong, attenuated lines.

This pronounced linear quality in his painting, which translated easily to various forms of printmaking, is especially characteristic of our portrait, a lithograph, of Delius. The circumstances surrounding the creation of this print are not known precisely. It was probably done in 1922, in conjunction with a biography of Delius being prepared by Dr. Heinrich Simon, owner of the *Frankfurter Zeitung*. The biography, which was never written, was to have been published by Reinhard Piper (of Piper Verlag, Munich), who later that same year also requested Beckmann to make a likeness of Delius.

Frederick Delius *by Max Beckmann (1922), lithograph, 65.5 × 38.5 cm, Kunstsammlungen der Veste Coburg, Coburg, Germany*

Richard Strauss

In this portrait, we find one great artist acknowledging another. Richard Strauss (1864–1949) had high regard for the aging Max Liebermann (1847–1935), who created at least four different studies of the composer (two oils, one etching, one lithograph). In our portrait, Liebermann adopted a subdued palette. He also tightened his brushwork to eliminate most traces of German expressionism that had crept into his painting at the beginning of the First World War. With uncanny instinct, the artist managed to bring out the serious and sedate side of his sitter. Here is the same bourgeois gentleman that Strauss was in private life, and whose ideal he raised to the level of high art in his music.

The year 1918, in which Liebermann painted Strauss, proved a turning point for both artists. One of Germany's most honored painters, Max Liebermann found himself in strained financial circumstances at the end of the war. Earlier in life, he had experimented with certain nineteenth-century traditions, including those of the Barbizon School and impressionism. But the difficult times brought on by the war compelled him to fall back on a more naturalistic style of painting to provide a living for himself.

Strauss, on the other hand, had come to the end of a twenty-year tenure as conductor of the Berlin Opera, which he served under a variety of different titles. He was about to move to Vienna, where he would assume the position of joint director of the newly reorganized Vienna Staatsoper. At least in its initial stages, this appointment was marked by considerable controversy. Three months before his new position became official, the premier of his *Die Frau ohne Schatten* was given at the Staatsoper. The cast of that initial performance reads as though drawn from the ranks of immortals: Lotte Lehmann as the dyer's wife, Maria Jeritza as the empress, Richard Mayr as Barak. Despite these able voices, the first production of *Frau* fell short of success, largely because of difficulties in staging and because of the overtly symbolic nature of the story which turns on human ideals of unselfishness and fertility.

Strauss was at the height of his powers as conductor and composer when Liebermann's portrait was painted. Greatly influenced by the harmonies and orchestration of Wagner, the composer had first established a name for himself as a master of orchestral color with the performance of his tone poem, *Don Juan*, in Weimar in late 1889. A bare six months later, that reputation was solidified with the premier of *Tod und Verklärung*. At the same time, Strauss had also begun work on the first of his operas. It was not until his one-act *Salome* was first performed in 1905 that he achieved true recognition in opera, the medium that was to dominate the second half of his career. *Elektra, Der Rosenkavalier, Ariadne auf Naxos*, and *Die Frau ohne Schatten* followed his initial foray into opera at two- to four-year intervals.

In 1918, Strauss had already begun *Intermezzo*, which would mark a dramatic change in direction from the vast romantic and allegorical spectacle of *Frau. Intermezzo* possessed a new, more naturalistic style, characteristic of postwar German art and theater. Based on an episode from the composer's life, its libretto was completed by Strauss just before he sat for Liebermann.

At the end of the war, Max Liebermann was also working in a considerably more controlled, detailed manner. This is ironic, for earlier the artist was influenced by the works of the French realists, Courbet and Manet, and by the seventeenth-century Dutch master Franz Hals. Inspired by these artists, Liebermann adopted a technique of loose brushwork and a dark palette which he reserved for the subjects of these years. In the 1890s he would become so attracted to more contemporary French painting that by the turn of the century he was known as a leading German impressionist.

Liebermann achieved his reputation largely from his representations of contemporary life. Like Lenbach, who painted portraits of Clara Schumann (pp. 94f.) and Edvard Grieg (pp. 108f.), he was also one of the most popular portraitists of his day. His sitters represent a cross-section of German intellectuals, artists, and literati. In 1899 he was elected president of the newly formed Berlin Secession, a loose alliance of artists of more contemporary persuasion. Two years after this portrait of Richard Strauss was done, Liebermann would be elected president of the Prussian Academy.

Richard Strauss *by Max Liebermann (1918), oil on canvas, 135 × 101 cm, Staatliche Museen zu Berlin*

Jean Sibelius

Before all else, the name Jean Sibelius (1865–1957) brings to mind an image of nature that is inevitably tied to the composer's native Finland. Mist, snow, long nights, returning swans, and the coming of spring are all subjects employed by Sibelius that might initially be considered the province of the poet or painter.

This portrait of young Jean Sibelius is compelling because of some simple devices used with dramatic effect by the painter, Akseli Gallen-Kallela (1865–1931). With a look of intensity in his eyes, the composer stares into space to the side of the composition, perhaps considering a musical idea. His jaw is set, his hair unkempt. His eyes are focused, but they engage nothing. Gallen-Kallela must have known this contemplative side of Sibelius intimately. Both men had participated in gatherings of a group of artists, the Symposium, for almost two years.

The period from which Gallen's portrait of Sibelius comes is sometimes called by the same name, his Symposium period (1892–1895). The term derives from a small group of artists, writers, and musicians who gathered in Helsinki around the Finnish painter, Gallen-Kallela, and the equally famous Sibelius. Much like Parisian artists of the nineteenth century, members of the group met in restaurants (the *Kämp* being one of their favorites) to discuss, in Sibelius's words, "the most diverse questions but always in an optimistic and revolutionary spirit. The way was to be cleared for new ideas in all fields" (Ringbom, 41).

Inspired by these evenings of artistic camaraderie, Gallen painted two versions of the same scene—members of the Symposium (the painter and Sibelius among them) seated at a table replete with glasses and liquor bottles. One of their number is asleep at the end of the table. Others look off into the distance with eyes glazed over either in inspiration or inebriation. The second, more finished version of the first was called *The Problem*. When displayed in Helsinki in 1894, it produced a storm of protest from bourgeois art lovers, one of whom proposed rechristening the work "The Mistake."

Gallen's and Sibelius's careers were linked even before the group was formed. In 1889, both received grants from the state to study abroad. At the time, Gallen was already established in Paris where he had displayed scenes of Finnish peasant life in 1888. There, he gradually became aware of the work of the post-impressionists, Gauguin and Van Gogh foremost among them. Like Sibelius, Gallen was moved by Finnish national songs. He commented that the poetry of national epics like the *Kalevala* made a decisive "contribution to my efforts to find both in Nature and in the people the forms of beauty that reflect unimpaired originality and primeval force" (Nordenson, 135).

The accompanying portrait of Jean Sibelius is a detail from an uncompleted triptych entitled *Jean Sibelius, Composer of En Saga*. *En Saga* was one of Sibelius's great orchestral scores, first performed in February 1893 with the composer conducting. Because of its title, the piece has been said to derive from various Finnish and international epics. Almost fifty years after *En Saga* was written, Sibelius denied these literary associations, claiming the composition reflected instead a state of mind. Whatever the case, the symphonic poem has impressed critics as both mythical and reminiscent of nature.

Gallen's watercolor portrait of Sibelius occupies the upper right third of the triptych. There is only one other completed portion of the triptych, a fantasy landscape (not reproduced here) found in the upper left corner. In spirit this scene derives only loosely from Sibelius's *En Saga*. It features a stream and castle, a fruit tree in the foreground, and flakes of falling snow. This portion of the triptych bears definite similarity to Japanese prints, which Gallen must have seen in Paris. Even more graphically, it reflects the inspiration of Gauguin. The remaining panel of the triptych, a thin blank field in the lower left, was never executed. It was to have contained a musical quotation from *En Saga*, which Sibelius had been asked to supply. But the composer failed to fulfill the painter's request.

Jean Sibelius,
Composer of "En Saga"
*by Akseli Gallen-Kallela
(1894), watercolor, 31 ×
17 cm (detail) Ainola, The
Jean Sibelius Museum,
Järvenpää*

Ferruccio Busoni

The artistic relationship between Ferruccio Busoni and Umberto Boccioni was indeed a fascinating one. Both men were among the leaders in their respective art forms in the Italian avant-garde just after the turn of the century. Both were possessed by a respect for the past which they sought to revivify in their art. Both were brilliant theorists. Both might be called true futurists. It is small wonder the affinity between them was so strong.

As its name implies, futurism was an artistic and literary movement which sought to bring Italy into the twentieth century. It had flourished less than three years when Busoni (1866–1924) first became aware of it in 1912. The composer and talented pianist was in London on a concert tour while the first exhibition of futurist art to visit England was being displayed at the Sackville Gallery. There, Busoni at once recognized the merit of Boccioni's work and was drawn to the pioneering spirit of his fellow countryman, even though Boccioni (1882–1916) was a generation younger than the composer.

Boccioni and Busoni met later that same year, apparently for the first time. Busoni was in Berlin, where he made his home, when the great 1912 Futurist Exhibition reached that city. The composer, who possessed a discriminating eye, bought one of Boccioni's most venturesome canvases, *The City Rises*, which came to Berlin with the exhibition. This modern urban study of color, light, and motion was the first truly large-scale painting evincing pure futurist ideals. Boccioni and Filippo Marinetti (the founder and chief theoretician of the movement) also called on Busoni and had a spirited discussion with the musician. Busoni hung his new painting in his music room where it, in part, inspired the surging, magical quality of the composer's largely atonal Second Sonatina.

While later Busoni grew cautious about futurist ideas, he maintained a friendship with Boccioni that lasted until the latter's untimely death in the war. The musician had wanted his portrait painted by the young futurist but had to wait until 1916. That year saw Busoni recently returned from a discouraging, nine-month concert tour of the United States. Once back on the Continent, he settled in Zurich, where, once again, he plunged into another series of concerts. Given this dizzying schedule, an invitation from the Marchese Casanova to visit the Marchese's hilltop Villa of San Remigo on Lake Maggiore must have come as welcome relief to Busoni. It was here that he finished work on his *Arlecchino*, which had occupied him since 1914. Though the short, comic opera is rarely performed today, the composer regarded it as his most satisfying work.

At the same time Boccioni was serving as a cyclist in the Italian army. On leave from the war, he traveled to the Marchese Casanova's villa at San Remigo. It was there that he painted two of his final canvases, the individual portraits of Ferruccio and Gerda Busoni. Since completing *The City Rises*, Boccioni had become increasingly interested in combining aspects of cubism with futurism. This interest in cubism led the Italian artist to examine the work of Paul Cézanne, one of the greatest influences on the cubists.

All this helps explain the rather atypical nature of Boccioni's *Portrait of Ferruccio Busoni*. Here, Boccioni has come under the influence of Cézanne rather dramatically. The blues, lavenders, and browns in the *Busoni* are drawn directly from the palette of the late Cézanne. Likewise, the treatment of the lake in the background is strikingly similar to that found in Cézanne's *Lake at Annecy* (1896).

By no means should Boccioni's debt to Cézanne detract from the impressive quality of this portrait. If anything, it enhances the imposing physical stature that was one of Busoni's chief physical characteristics during these years. The artist insisted on setting the portrait outdoors. Busoni rests casually on a balustrade, looking imperiously down at the viewer. With this pose, Boccioni captured something of the prowess, perhaps even hauteur, of the composer of the demonic opera *Doctor Faust*, the author of *Wesen und Einheit der Musik*.

Boccioni returned to his unit after an idyllic month of painting at San Remigo. He would die that summer at the age of thirty-four, the result of injuries sustained when he fell from a horse during military maneuvers. Ironically, Busoni commemorated his friend, not through music, but in an article about the artist that appeared on the front page of the *Neue Zürcher Zeitung*.

Ferruccio Busoni *by Umberto Boccioni (1916), oil on canvas, 170 × 126 cm, Galleria Nazionale d'Arte Moderna, Rome*

Erik Satie

In our age, the greatest audacity is simplicity.
COCTEAU ABOUT SATIE'S MUSIC

Paris in the early twentieth century was the center of a vigorous artistic life, as it had been at the time of Chopin and Delacroix. Shortly before 1900, Paris had witnessed a tremendous surge of development in industry and technology, among other fields. These developments accounted in part for the *Expositions Universelles* in 1878, 1889, and 1900. Cinematography arrived on the French scene (1895); cabarets and music halls flourished (*Le Chat Noir*, 1883; *Moulin Rouge*, 1889); new concert organizations were founded.

As at the time of Victor Hugo and Berlioz, the avant-garde set the tone. Artists in different fields interacted and inspired each other. The cafés in which they now met may have been different ones, and the subjects discussed covered a broader spectrum, partly because new artistic media, such as film, had been established. But now as then, professional collaborations and personal friendships resulted in portraits of and by some of the leading artists of the time.

Picasso's pencilled portrait of Erik Satie (1866–1925), done in 1920, grew from such collaboration. Here we see, as in other works of the time, a change in preferred media. Fewer portraits were done in oil, while lithographs and drawings increased in popularity. Traditional realism gave way to newer styles such as cubism and fauvism.

Satie was a composer who, in his life and works, exemplifies this close interrelation of the arts. Indeed, some painters viewed Satie as a "Picasso of music" (Gowers, 519), for both had broken away from impressionism. The young Satie had been a friend of Debussy, the latter acting often as helper and adviser. But musically they went different ways.

Satie's style was antiromantic as well as anti-impressionistic. The strange, nonsensical titles of some of his compositions (*Pieces in the Shape of a Pear; Cold Pieces*) suggest ties to dadaism, a rather shortlived movement espousing the importance of instinct rather than intellect as an artistic driving force. Dada appealed to Satie; a leader of the movement, Francis Picabia, became one of Satie's close friends and made a drawing of the composer in 1924. Satie himself was a draftsman not without talent; many of his music manuscripts and letters contain illustrations.

Among the most innovative manifestations of the performing arts, especially in Paris, was the ballet, and it was in this art form that Satie's and Picasso's paths crossed. Around the years of World War I, it brought together artists from many lands—dancers, musicians, and stage and costume designers among them. Those who contributed to the development of modern (now quite different from classic) ballet were major artists who had come to hospitable Paris. The name of the outstanding company, the Ballets Russes, reminds us of the origin of some: Igor Stravinsky, composer; Serge Diaghilev, impresario; Léonide Massine, dancer and choreographer. The Spanish painter Pablo Picasso had arrived in Paris in 1900; he remained one of the strongest personalities to influence the course of modern art in general. Through his designs of scenery, drop curtains, and costumes he gave distinction to some of the best known ballets of the time, including several with Satie's music.

Picasso designed sets and drop curtains for *Parade*, a collaboration between Jean Cocteau (see pp. 148f.) and Satie, produced by Diaghilev. Massine was the choreographer. *Parade*'s opening on May 18, 1917, caused a scandal to which Satie reacted with rage.

Picasso's portrait of Satie is dated May 19, 1920, soon after their collaboration on *Parade*. Later that year it was reproduced in the program booklet for the Ballets Russes. Their friendship was to continue. In the year before Satie's death, Picasso designed scenery and costumes for his friend's ballet, *Mercure*.

The portrait is part of an informal series of 1920 which included very similar line drawings of Stravinsky and de Falla. A similar portrait of Léon Bakst, (painter, designer of costumes and sets for Diaghilev) dates from 1922. Though Picasso's Satie definitely is a likeness—a representational, realistic portrait—it does convey an impression of directness, squareness, and heaviness (note the composer's hands) not uncommon in other Picasso works from this period. Yet we may also see reflected here the simplicity, the economy of Satie's musical means, that prompted Cocteau's aphorism at the beginning of this essay (quoted in Peters, 54), as well as the linearity of Satie's music which reminded Cocteau of Ingres.

In 1925 Jean Cocteau, one of France's most distinguished writers of plays, essays, and scenarios for film and other media, also sketched Satie. By the time Satie met Cocteau in 1915, the latter was well established in artistic and intellectual circles and in Paris society. Having heard Satie's *Pieces in the Shape of a Pear*, Cocteau was inspired to collaborate with the composer. As we noted above, the scenario for *Parade* resulted.

Satie intrigued other portraitists as well. We have mentioned Picabia. Suzanne Valadon, mother of the painter Maurice Utrillo and her-

Erik Satie *by Pablo Picasso (1920), pencil on gray paper, 62.3 × 48 cm, Musée Picasso, Paris*

self a painter, has left us an oil portrait of Satie dating approximately from 1892. Their love affair—probably his only one, though one of many for her—lasted but a few years.

Finally, one might add that Satie's tomb was designed by his friend Constantin Brancusi, a major sculptor of the time, who had come to Paris from Bucharest in 1904. He remained Satie's close friend to the end.

Arnold Schoenberg

Much has been written about Schoenberg (1874–1951) and his place in twentieth-century music. "Atonal," "twelve-tone," or "serial" composition are labels commonly attached to his styles of several periods. Like most labels of this kind, they are less-than-satisfactory generalizations. Writers usually stress the controversial aspects of his music, including the negative, often violent audience reactions. In doing so, these commentators tend to overlook Schoenberg's background in traditional music, reflected in his great admiration of Mahler.

Schoenberg taught music theory at a Berlin conservatory; he had moved there in 1901. Upon returning to Vienna two years later he taught at a private school which also counted Oskar Kokoschka among its faculty members.

Schoenberg's lifelong interest in painting is reflected in his contacts and friendships with artists who formed the avant-garde during the early decades of this century. Among painters, Wassily Kandinsky then had achieved a position of prominence comparable to that of Schoenberg in music. Both were concerned with esthetics, with theory, with the function of art in society. These concerns transcended their respective disciplines, as is amply documented by the Schoenberg-Kandinsky correspondence.

Many of Schoenberg's compositions met with extremely hostile audience reactions. Perhaps his disappointments and frustrations—his inability to "get through" to the majority of his listeners—were among the factors that caused him to take up painting as another creative outlet. The years from 1907–1911 saw him intensively involved with that art form, resulting in approximately seventy oil paintings. According to Freitag's catalog, thirteen of these are self portraits. Others represent musicians, Mahler and Alban Berg among them. He also painted landscapes and fairly abstract subjects he called "visions" or "gazes." Their style (not surprisingly) reflects the expressionism of the artists with whom he associated. His frustrations as a composer may account for two paintings entitled *The Critic*, and for an allegorial painting, *Hatred*.

Great intensity of emotion, an agonized, contorted quality, characterizes much of his painting, as it does his music from the same period. Color, in the normal, visual, sense of that word, and tone color, play a crucial part in his work; at times both converge in one composition. Thus the vocal score of his "drama with music" *Die glückliche Hand* (The Lucky Hand, 1910–1913) abounds with detailed stage direc-

tions referring to color: to "a dark, violet curtain," "greenish light." A "light crescendo... begins with dull red light... that turns to brown and then a dirty green" (Hahl-Koch, 91–92). Schoenberg provided numerous sketches (oil, watercolor, crayon) to clarify his intentions.

A major exhibition of Schoenberg's paintings took place in 1910. Kandinsky showed many of them in the *Blue Rider* exhibition of 1911, including a self portrait of that year.

Schoenberg's painting reproduced here is known as the "Blue Self Portrait," to distinguish it from other, somewhat similar ones, emphasizing green or brownish tones, all painted at approximately the same time. Both the "blue" and the "green" (1910) show the composer's face only—a straight, frontal view. The color in our self portrait is more intense than in the green one, and the definition of form is fairly linear, with clear contours set off from a background of distinctly different color. The green portrait appears more hazy and mysterious, closer in mood to some of Schoenberg's "visions." As in all his portraits, the facial expression and general mood are serious, intense.

In a 1950 interview with the composer Halsey Stevens, Schoenberg pointed out that painting, to him, was the same as composing—"a way of expressing myself, of presenting emotions, ideas" (Stevens, 109; see also Alban Berg, pp. 140f.).

The Austrian painter Oskar Kokoschka (1886–1980) also is associated with expressionism, though he usually painted from nature. Indeed the many landscapes and cityscapes, painted throughout his career, brought him special recognition. As a painter and as a playwright, he contributed much that was controversial. His paintings attracted the interest of Kandinsky in Munich, around the time of the first *Blue Rider* exhibition. Schoenberg and Kokoschka met before that. In 1913 Schoenberg recommended Kokoschka as the artist best suited for a collaboration on a (silent!) film version of *Die glückliche Hand*, involving not only coloration of the film but using light reflectors in the theater.

During his long, distinguished career Kokoschka maintained friendships with many musicians, saying that he had more satisfying relations with musicians than with painters or

Arnold Schoenberg, Self Portrait (1910), oil on wood, 31 × 22 cm, Arnold Schoenberg Institute, The University of Southern California, Los Angeles

129

writers. His lively interest in music (he attended the first performance of Berg's *Wozzeck*) and musicians resulted in several portraits: that of the composer Anton Webern (1914, see pp. 138f.); the cellist Pablo Casals (1954, "a short, robust man whom I could hardly see behind his large instrument"); Michael Tippett (1963); and Arnold Schoenberg. He was asked to paint Arturo Toscanini, the conductor, but decided against it.

It is a measure of Kokoschka's stature that he was asked, or allowed, to paint important figures from many walks of life, among them the poet Ezra Pound, German ex-chancellor Konrad Adenauer, and German president Theodor Heuss. His friendship with the conductor Wilhelm Furtwängler led to Kokoschka's designing a production of Mozart's *Magic Flute* for the Salzburg Festival of 1955.

Kokoschka's portrait of Schoenberg dates from 1924 when the painter returned to Vienna from Dresden. He visited the composer at his residence in Mödling near Vienna, painting him in the act of playing chamber music with some of his pupils. No instrument is visible, but the positions of hands and arms are clearly those involved in playing the cello. Though expressionistic in its heavy brushwork and use of strong color (chiefly dark blues and greens), it is a fairly realistic portrait—it is, as said earlier, based on the artist's observing his subject, on "seeing." Indeed Kokoschka founded a *Schule des Sehens* (school of seeing) in 1953, a summer academy in Salzburg which he directed for eleven years.

Arnold Schoenberg *by Oskar Kokoschka (1924), oil on canvas, c. 97 × 75 cm, private collection*

131

Manuel de Falla

Once more Paris was the setting that stimulated the collaboration of two major non-French artists. Manuel de Falla (1876–1946) was born in Cádiz in southern Spain; throughout his career as a composer he drew inspiration from the sights and sounds, from the folklore, history, and scenery of his native Andalusia. Pablo Picasso (1881–1973) came from the same region, having been born in Málaga.

In spite of these strong roots, the young composer, after early studies at home and in Madrid, was eager to go to Paris. He arrived there in 1907 and stayed until war broke out in 1914. They were years he always considered unforgettable. In Paris he was to make acquaintances and establish friendships with many musicians, Debussy, Dukas, and Ravel among them, but also with artists in other fields. Debussy in particular became a friend who encouraged Falla and helped him in having his music performed. After Debussy's death, Falla composed the first of his *Homenajes* (homages) in his honor. The piece includes a brief quotation from Debussy's *Evening in Granada*. The contacts and friendships Falla established during the Paris years led to commissions and collaborations long after he had returned to Spain.

Nights in the Gardens of Spain, a fantasy for piano and orchestra, was begun in Paris but completed and first performed in Madrid in 1916. At this time another work, also among his most beloved today, was conceived, a mimed comedy or *farsa* about the corregidor and the miller's wife. When Diaghilev and his choreographer Massine listened to Falla's score they were most enthusiastic and commissioned him to compose a larger version, using full orchestra. They had just discovered a wonderful flamenco dancer in Madrid whom they wanted to introduce to London audiences with this ballet, which became known in English as *The Three-Cornered Hat*. This is where Picasso entered.

Like Manuel de Falla, Pablo Picasso had visited Paris early in life, for the first time in 1900. Unlike the composer he made his home in France until his death. Two years after collaborating with Satie and Cocteau on *Parade* (see p. 126), Picasso joined Diaghilev's troupe in London, to prepare the 1919 performance of *The Three-Cornered Hat*, designing a drop curtain, sets, and costumes. It was a successful production that brought much acclaim to both Falla and Picasso. The following year it was given in Paris. Cabanne gives a lively description of the lavish supper given in honor of the two artists after the first Paris performance. Picasso proclaimed that Falla was the real guest of honor; jokingly he insisted that a laurel wreath be painted on the composer's bald pate.

During this year, 1920, Picasso made several other pencil drawings in the style of the Falla portrait. Stravinsky and Satie (see p. 127) are drawn in very much the same pose and manner: even the chair in which they sit is the same in all three drawings. They are lifelike, in a typical, fairly heavy, bold Picasso style that is entirely different from his cubist paintings of the preceding decade. Their lean, linear qualities rather suggest the artist's emerging neoclassic manner.

In Picasso's pencilled portrait, de Falla looks sturdy and determined. He was short, but the perspective chosen by Picasso conceals this.

During these years Picasso created a number of similar line drawings. Some, it is thought, were requested by his friends, the poets Louis Aragon, André Breton, and Jean Cocteau. There is a line drawing of Diaghilev from 1919.

Years later, the composer Francis Poulenc reminisced about his friendship with Manuel de Falla and about their last period of working together, at the Venice Festival of 1932. He provided a brief but loving verbal portrait of the great Spanish musician, remembering him as a meticulous worker, and as a human being of great modesty with a profound, mystical faith.

Manuel de Falla by Pablo Picasso (1920), pencil on gray paper, c. 62 × 48 cm, Musée Picasso, Paris

Carl Ruggles

The "Sun-Treader" in this portrait's title derives from Carl Ruggles's longest composition, a single-movement tone poem of the same title, composed between 1926 and 1931. The rising and falling lines of the piece echo the stride of the Sun-Treader, a term which Ruggles (1876–1971) borrowed from Browning's epithet for Shelley.

> Sun-treader—life and light be thine for ever;
> Thou art gone from us—years go by—and spring
> Gladdens, and the young earth is beautiful,
> Yet thy songs come not—other bards arise
> But none like thee . . .
>
> ROBERT BROWNING, *PAULINE*

Intense chromaticism and touches of a distinctive, personal atonality make Ruggles's *"The Sun-Treader"* (along with other examples of the composer's mature music) highly individualistic. While Ruggles knew the work of Berg, Varèse, and Ives, he gave his compositions his own individual stamp.

Our portrait of Ruggles by Thomas Hart Benton (1889–1975) contains features common to composers' portraits going back to the baroque: keyboard instrument, musical manuscript, composer. Benton combined these characteristics in a manner, however, that is unmistakably regionalist. Perhaps the most telling feature in this regard is the grand piano that, contrary to the principles of foreshortening, seems to swell in size toward the rear. The perspective of the floorboards is forced, the floor itself is tilted up, and the bench is angled toward the piano to create the effect of a charged, rushing space. Benton treats Ruggles's clothing with characteristic simplicity but exaggerates the contours of his subject's body, and especially those of his face. These animate undulations might easily be construed as a caricature of Ruggles. Photographs of the composer, however, reveal a face that is every bit as strongly contoured as Benton's portrait.

Thomas Hart Benton is among the most popular and vilified American artists of the twentieth century. In part this stems from the outspoken opinions the irascible artist expressed freely in his many writings, in particular his two autobiographies, *An Artist in America* and *An American in Art.*

Benton was the most vocal of the artists in the "regionalist" tradition. By his own account, the term was first coined in the late 1920s to describe a number of artists—Charles Burchfield, Edward Hopper, Grant Wood, and John Steuart Curry. Along with Benton, these artists painted recognizably American subjects, especially scenes of life drawn from the Midwest. In selecting this type of subject matter, Benton turned his back on ideas he regarded as European, ideas that had led him to paint in an abstract manner during World War I.

The year 1934, in which he painted the portrait of Carl Ruggles, found Benton preparing to move back to his native Missouri. At that time the artist had lived in New York for more than twenty years. Since 1926, he had been taking trips through the rural South and Midwest, which convinced him of the validity of western subject matter. In truth, Benton had also tired of New York, its politics, its intellectualism, its overcrowded conditions, and critical opinion against his work.

Benton's interest in painting musical scenes dates from the first of these journeys of discovery to the American heartland. Outside Jasper, Arkansas, the artist drew "a genuine Ozark fiddler" (Marling, 4). Almost fifty years later, that same figure still inspired the country musicians depicted in Benton's paintings. Until the end of World War II, Benton's musical tastes remained genuinely populist. Sections of his paintings—indeed entire scenes—were turned over to American music: hoedowns, gospel music, burlesque, music hall, and jazz.

In part, this choice of identifiable, popular American musical idioms represented the painter's backlash against the cultural establishment of the East Coast, and New York City in particular. But inspiring this attraction perhaps most immediately was Tom Benton, the musician.

Though tone deaf, he taught himself to play the harmonica. By the early 1930s he had formed "Tom Benton and His Harmonica Boys," a group of friends, varied in number and talent, who played fiddle, banjo, guitar, accordion, and flute. They gathered to practice and entertain friends with folk and popular favorites at apartments in New York and at neighbors' homes on Martha's Vineyard where the Bentons vacationed.

Given the painter's musical predilections at the time, it might seem strange that he should choose to represent a composer of the American classical avant-garde. Benton recalled that he got to know Ruggles, along with Edgard Varèse (see p. 142), in the 1920s at artistic soirees given by friends in New York. In the autumn of 1933, Ruggles invited his painter friend to visit him at his home in Arlington, Vermont. While there, Benton made sketches of his host at the piano, which he reworked into the painting of 1934. Benton thought it one of the best portraits he ever made.

'The Sun-Treader''—Portrait of Carl Ruggles *by Thomas Hart Benton (1934), egg tempera on canvas, 113.3 ×
96.5 cm, Nelson-Atkins Museum of Art, Kansas City*

Igor Stravinsky

Stravinsky's portrait by Robert Delaunay has recently been shown. The canvas has created a sensation; it is certainly not flattering, but at any rate it is expressive.

It was Tristan Tzara, the Rumanian writer and a founder of the dada movement, who made this observation in a 1922 edition of *Vanity Fair*.

Today it is difficult to understand why the painting caused such a reaction. In it, Robert Delaunay (1885–1941) adopted an unusually high point of view, which compels the viewer to look down over the composer's shoulder. This particular vantage point strengthens the lines of Igor Stravinsky's (1882–1971) long, angular face. Delaunay employs certain highly tempered cubist devices in the geometrical treatment of his subject's nose, his chin, and the back of his head. Likewise, the lines of his clothing have been simplified and flattened. This allowed the artist to work with pure color, a chief characteristic of his style. Here, unsaturated primary and secondary colors are used to emphasize various flattened planes that make up the sitter's body.

Along with other of Stravinsky's portraitists (Goncharova, Larinov, Picasso), Delaunay was himself the founder of an early modern art movement, in his case, Orphism, an offshoot of the cubist tradition. The artist believed in the use of chromatic, or "prismatic" color, one of Orphism's chief characteristics. As early as 1912, this led him to paint in a manner that all but eliminated recognizable objects. By the time he did the *Stravinsky*, however, Delaunay had returned to painting in a more naturalistic fashion. Similarly, Stravinsky had begun working in a loosely neoclassical idiom in *Pulcinella*, the last ballet he composed for Diaghilev before Delaunay painted this portrait.

Robert and Sonia Delaunay had first come to know Diaghilev when the couple was living in Spain during World War I. There they had become enamored of Spanish folk scenes and, with the Ballets Russes choreographer Léonide Massine, had conceived a production inspired by Spanish dance. While this project was never mounted, the Delaunays did the sets and some costumes for a revival of *Cleopatra*. Diaghilev originally created this ballet in 1909 to a pastiche of improbable pieces drawn from the music of no fewer than seven Russian composers. Delaunay was to replace the original sets by Leon Bakst, which had burned. Sonia Delaunay was asked to supplement costumes by Bakst. These various borrowings account, in part, for the revival's lack of success. Delaunay's colorful, cubist sets, which featured brilliantly colored pyramids, further alienated critics. Delaunay planned other projects with the Ballets Russes; none was ever realized.

The Russian impresario, Serge Diaghilev, was responsible for Delaunay's painting Stravinsky's portrait in Madrid in April 1921. In that year, Diaghilev also brought together Matisse and Prokofiev for the same purpose (see pp. 144f.). Stravinsky had begun his great collaboration with Diaghilev much earlier, in 1909. They would work together until the impresario's death twenty years later. In that space of time, Stravinsky composed no fewer than ten scores for the Ballets Russes. The first of these was the *Firebird*, which was presented in Paris in 1910, followed in rapid succession by *Petrushka* in 1911, the *Rite of Spring* in 1913, and the *Nightingale* in 1914. It was on the sets for the revision of *Nightingale* that Matisse would work later in the decade. After *Nightingale*, the pace of Stravinsky's work for Diaghilev fell off, but only slightly.

Owing in large part to his association with Diaghilev, Stravinsky made many brief friendships with artists. He would comment about Delaunay to Robert Craft, his assistant and friend:

> He talked too much and too enthusiastically about "modern art," but otherwise was quite likeable. He did a portrait of me too. I don't know what has become of it, but it was certainly better than Albert Gleizes' cubist one, which is my mustache plus what-have-you.... Delaunay was often with [Diaghilev], and in Madrid, in 1921, we were all three constantly together. (Stravinsky and Craft, 113)

Perhaps no twentieth-century composer has had his portrait done as frequently and by as diverse a set of artists as Stravinsky. In addition to Delaunay, Jacques-Emile Blanche (see pp. 150f.), Albert Gleizes, Natalie Goncharova, and Michail Larinov painted Stravinsky. Alberto Giacometti and Pablo Picasso (see pp. 132f.) drew him frequently. Marino Marini sculpted him. The long list of famous photographers who took his picture includes Richard Avedon, Henri Cartier-Bresson, Man Ray, and Edward Weston.

The great number of portraits of Stravinsky is all the more unusual because so much of the role that painting and sculpture played in portraiture in the nineteenth century has been taken over by the camera in the twentieth. Stravinsky's popularity among artists was due in large part to his contribution to modern music, and to his ensuing fame. But almost as pilgrims to Mecca, artists also gravitated to Stravinsky because of his fascinating face. Its gaunt, aquiline features offered them a great deal to work with in attempting to provide new visual solutions to the age-old problem of portraiture.

Igor Stravinsky by Robert Delaunay (1921), oil on canvas, 65.5 × 54 cm, Walsall Museum and Art Gallery, Walsall, England

Anton Webern

Many important early twentieth-century artists were influenced by music: Braque, Kandinsky, Klee, Klimt, Kokoschka, Mondrian, Picasso. The list could also include the Austrian painter, Max Oppenheimer (1885–1954). Born in Vienna, Oppenheimer (called "Mopp") attended the academy in his native city and in Prague before beginning his artistic career. From his youth he possessed a strong love of music.

In 1909, Oppenheimer painted a haunting portrait of Arnold Schoenberg who appears overcome with fear and suspicion. It was through Schoenberg and the painter's own participation in the famous Cassirer Circle that Oppenheimer came into contact with other Viennese composers and intellectuals. Over a twenty-year period he represented Anton Webern (1908), Heinrich (1911) and Thomas Mann (1926), Ferruccio Busoni (1916), Peter Attenberg, and Arthur Schnitzler.

In addition, one of his most ambitious undertakings, *Orchestra* (1921–23), was inspired by Gustav Mahler conducting a performance of *Des Knaben Wunderhorn*. Mopp also painted smaller ensembles, including a representation entitled *String Quartet* (1916) in which he showed nothing but the performers' hands, music, and instruments. The style for this particular piece (as the *Busoni* of the same year) would have to be called a hybrid of expressionism and cubism. Hands are shown elongated, almost tortured. Instruments and music are flattened and turned on radical angles. Space is crowded, filled to the point of being claustrophobic. It is easy to imagine the quartet playing Schoenberg's String Quartet No. 2, or Webern's own *Six Bagatelles.*

The style which Oppenheimer used in his 1908 portrait of Anton Webern (1883–1945) was unabashedly expressionistic, in the true Viennese sense of the term. This particular idiom was adopted for composers' portraits as early as 1906 by Richard Gerstl, who painted a singularly uncompromising portrait of Arnold Schoenberg. Oppenheimer followed shortly thereafter with his own portrait of the same awkward, self-conscious composer.

By the time he painted Webern's portrait, Oppenheimer had mastered expressionism. He astutely avoided a frontal, centralized point of view in setting up his composition. Instead Webern is posed on a rather radical angle, head at the top of the painting, eyes level with the viewer. His left shoulder slopes unnaturally, so that the artist has seemingly adopted two vantage points from which to assay his subject.

A solitary figure off to one side of the composition, Webern seems pitted against the totally blank surrounding field. A thin, irregular shadow of white encompasses his body. This spectral glow seems at once to eat away at the composer, and to provide him with a true expressionist aura. The lines of the body, face, and hands are especially tortured. There are none of the normal musical accessories here, and without them it is impossible to tell from the portrait alone that the subject is a musician. He has every appearance of being a serious thinker, however. In this Oppenheimer has successfully captured Webern, the intellectual and theorist.

Like Oppenheimer's portrait, much of Webern's music of this period has been termed expressionistic, perhaps inaccurately. Immediately preceding World War I, the Viennese painters Gustav Klimt, Oskar Kokoschka, and Egon Schiele sought new ways of painting that more adequately revealed political tensions in the crumbling Austro-Hungarian empire. Likewise, Anton Webern struggled to create a new musical language that represented a radical break from the lush, late romantic compositions of Brahms and Mahler.

At this time in his career, Webern was still influenced by Schoenberg. The younger composer had not completely broken the constraints of nineteenth-century tonality, but he had taken steps in that direction. His *Four Pieces*, Op. 7, of 1910, achieves a tension in harmony and melodic range that clearly parallels the psychological tensions Oppenheimer incorporated in this portrait. Webern, himself, certainly saw this. In April 1909, he wrote the artist a letter in which he reacted favorably to the unusual qualities of the portrait: "Hardly anything is more nauseating to me than the matter of fact attitude that the Philistine brings to a work of art" (Moldenhauer, 109–110). With this, Webern may have been steeling himself for the landslide of unfavorable criticism that was to greet his own work.

Anton Webern *by Max Oppenheimer (1908), oil on canvas, 80 × 70 cm, Von-der-Heydt-Museum, Wuppertal-Elberfeld, Germany*

Alban Berg

Perhaps the finest tribute to a musician is that paid by a fellow musician. In the case of Schoenberg's portrait of Berg, that tribute takes an unusual form, for it is visual rather than verbal, and done by Berg's famous mentor, Arnold Schoenberg (1874–1951). At the age of nineteen, Alban Berg (1885–1935) came to Schoenberg with little previous training in music. It was toward the end of Berg's apprenticeship as Schoenberg's student that this portrait was painted. Subsequently it was displayed in a show of the would-be painter's work held in Vienna in October 1910 by the book and art dealer Hugo Heller.

Schoenberg often emphasized that he was a self-taught artist. He might have begun painting as early as 1905, but he completed almost two-thirds of his work between 1908 and 1910. While Berg was his student between 1904 and 1910, Schoenberg's musical style progressed from the late nineteenth-century Viennese tonalism of his symphonic poem *Pelléas et Mélisande* to his abandonment of tonality in the great Second String Quartet. Shortly thereafter, he would develop *Sprechstimme*, a form of spoken singing, in *Die glückliche Hand*, begun in 1910. In other words, it was at precisely the time he rejected the harmonic basis of Western music that he was most active as a painter. Schoenberg explained the parallels between his painting and his music between 1908 and 1910 in this way:

> [Painting] was the same to me as making music. To me it was a way of expressing myself, of presenting emotions, ideas, and then other feelings.... I expressed myself in the same manner [in painting] as I did in music. I was never very capable of expressing my feelings or emotions in words. I do not know whether this is the reason for my doing so in music and also why I did it in painting or vice-versa. Because I had this as an outlet, I could renounce expressing something in words. (Stevens, 179)

Even though this analysis was offered by Schoenberg forty years after the portrait of Berg was executed, the sentiment contained in its words was in full accord with the spirit of German expressionism. Indeed, Schoenberg knew the expressionist painters Richard Gerstl, Wassily Kandinsky, and Oskar Kokoschka. It was the latter who introduced Schoenberg to the use of oils. Certainly the subjects of love and jealousy that characterize both Schoenberg's *Erwartung* and *Die glückliche Hand* are psychological, or expressionist, in nature.

The portrait of Alban Berg is clearly one of the most developed and naturalistic that Schoenberg was to do. Unlike the majority of the composer's paintings, the *Berg* boasts a fairly credible setting. The subject rests his right arm on a mantel; there is a landscape painting on the wall behind him and a doorway to the left. Expressionist features come out in the radical incline of the floor, in the angular lines of Berg's body, in its attenuated proportions, and in the portrait's unnaturalistic colors.

Later in life, Berg would compose *Wozzeck* (1925) and *Lulu,* on which the composer was working at the time of his sudden death. Today both are among the most frequently performed atonal operas in the repertoire. In them the composer employed certain expressionist devices that were earlier explored by such painters as Ernst Ludwig Kirchner, Kokoschka, and Emil Nolde. Among these expressionist qualities were Berg's penetrating psychological insight and his willingness to explore insanity and human depravity, all of which were applied to the development of his characters.

Berg himself was less venturesome at the time this portrait was painted. Through 1908, his student works (songs and a piano sonata) maintained a clearly tonal structure, though spiced with chromaticism. The last piece he wrote while a student of Schoenberg, String Quartet, Op. 3 (1910), however, reveals the touch of a composer who had mastered his own musical idiom. Then, as later in life, he was the same introspective person Schoenberg represented in this compelling portrait.

Alban Berg *by Arnold*
Schoenberg (c. 1910), oil
on canvas, 175.5 × 85 cm,
Historisches Museum der
Stadt Wien, Vienna

Edgard Varèse

Several years later Gaston Lachaise . . . did a head of Varèse—a beautiful likeness, though from one angle almost too faunlike to be the Varèse of those strenuous, stirring, indefatigable years. Did Lachaise sense the inner solitary Varèse, leaner than the exuberant extrovert. Or perhaps, that being the summer of 1927 when Varèse, suffering again from an old infection, (so the doctors said) may really have been as leanly handsome as Lachaise's portrait.

These words were written of our portrait by the person who knew Edgard Varèse (1883–1965) best at that time in his life, his wife, Louise (Varèse, 199). Indeed Gaston Lachaise (1882–1935) produced a striking translation of the composer's features into bronze. As a portraitist, the French sculptor possessed both an uncanny ability to perceive the underlying essentials of a sitter's face and the native talent to translate that image into three-dimensional form. To this Lachaise added an expressively modeled surface, derived in part from his exposure to impressionism, in part from his interest in the portraits of Rodin (see pp. 114f.), to capture the vitality of Varèse, the man and the composer.

The terms "electronic instruments," "noise," "sound masses," and "found music" have a very contemporary ring to them. Each is also associated with the music of Edgard Varèse. Though Varèse may not have been the first to employ these experimental techniques in every case, he was undoubtedly the composer whose music and ideas were responsible for introducing these newer, more philosophical notions to a generation of composers that now takes them for granted.

By his own choice, Varèse identified more readily with visual artists, and in particular with painters, than he did with fellow musicians. He often regarded the latter as more hidebound, more closely tied to traditional methods and thinking than his painter-friends: Fernand Léger, André Derain, Modigliani. When Varèse first came to the United States in 1916, he was attracted to the work of two avant-garde French artists then living in New York, Francis Picabia and Marcel Duchamp. Undoubtedly Duchamp's use of the ready-made and found objects encouraged Varèse's interest in incorporating commonplace sounds, or "noise," into his music. It is also clear that these visual artists were more than social acquaintances of Varèse; their ideas made a lasting mark on the developing composer.

There could be no happier alliance of composer and artist than that between Varèse and Gaston Lachaise. Also a French emigré, the sculptor came to the United States in 1906, a decade earlier than Varèse. He settled first in Boston, then moved to New York. Lachaise's favorite subject was the generously proportioned female nude. Next in quantity in his oeuvre were his exquisitely modeled portrait heads. The largest portion of these depicts individuals interested in the arts: writers, fellow artists, publishers, and patrons.

Lachaise met most of his subjects through Alfred Stieglitz's galleries—291 and the Intimate Gallery. He also found them through *The Dial* magazine, whose critic, Paul Rosenfeld, reviewed performances of Varèse's music in New York in the 1920s. Generally Lachaise's portraits have the more finished quality that is associated with the refined, burnished surfaces of his monumental nudes. Some, however, like that of the great American painter John Marin, and the *Varèse*, have a much more expressively rendered surface, which Lachaise may have somehow equated with the jarring, sometimes seemingly unfinished quality of both men's art.

It was through neither *The Dial* nor Stieglitz that Varèse and Lachaise met. As Louise Varèse tells the story, the two were first introduced at Romany Marie's, a little bistro in Greenwich Village that served as a rendezvous for artists of all kinds in the late 1920s. Stieglitz and Georgia O'Keeffe could be found there occasionally. Theodore Dreiser, Buckminster Fuller, Henry Miller, Paul Robeson, Carl Ruggles (see p. 134), and Mark Tobey were also among the habitués. There, too, Varèse came to know John Sloan, a leading member of the Ash Can School. In the mid-twenties, Sloan painted the composer seated in front of one of the instruments he developed for producing tonal vibrations electronically. Louise Varèse commented simply of Sloan's likeness of her husband, "He painted a very bad portrait of Varèse." Obviously, she felt more kindly toward the bronze by Lachaise.

Edgard Varèse by Gaston Lachaise, 1928–1930, bronze, 40 cm, Evansville Museum of Arts and Science, Evansville, Indiana

Serge Prokofiev

Four great names, among others, highlight the pages of the program for the 1921 Paris season of the Ballets Russes: Diaghilev, Massine, Matisse, and Prokofiev. That year the great Russian impresario, Serge Diaghilev, produced *The Tale of the Buffoon*, the first of Serge Prokofiev's ballets. Actually Diaghilev had commissioned the score six years earlier, but it was not to be performed until Prokofiev (1891–1953) traveled to France in 1921.

In the great tumult and aftermath of the Bolshevik Revolution, the young composer had left his native Russia for the United States. He was then only twenty-seven, a successful orchestral composer with two piano concertos, a concerto for violin, and his popular *Classical Symphony* behind him. On the long ocean voyage to the United States, he began composing his most durable opera, *The Love for Three Oranges*, which was subsequently commissioned by the Chicago Opera. Before it was performed, however, Prokofiev went to Paris where he revised *The Tale of the Buffoon* for Diaghilev. Henri Matisse (1869–1954) saw the ballet that same season and liked it.

Diaghilev was doing everything in his power to insure the success of the Russian composer's new ballet. Soon after his arrival in Paris, Prokofiev was dispatched to Nice by Diaghilev to sit for Matisse. While Prokofiev was there, Matisse made the sketch of the composer (opposite) for the cover of the Ballets Russes program. The original has disappeared. According to Boris Kochno, Diaghilev's secretary, it was rolled up and left in a hotel room after it had been reproduced for the cover.

To a degree, the drawing is uncharacteristic of Matisse, whose art was the epitome of simplicity. Here Matisse has included more detail and shading than is normal in his drawings, perhaps so the portrait would reproduce better. The constantly undulating lines found both in Prokofiev's clothing and in the outline of his face are fundamental to Matisse's work. They give the portrait an upward flow, culminating in Prokofiev's high, round forehead. When asked by Prokofiev why he had elongated the composer's head, Matisse is said to have responded, "Why, to give the feeling of your being very tall."

By 1909, when Matisse conceived his famous paintings *The Dance* and *Music*, the painter already nurtured a profound admiration for the ballet. It was not until 1919, however, that he was commissioned by Diaghilev to replace the decor and sets for Stravinsky's *Song of the Nightingale.*

The ballet had first been performed as the *Nightingale*, an operatic piece, in 1914, but the sets were lost during the war. Stravinsky revised the scenario and score of the last two acts in 1917, but *Song of the Nightingale,* as the revised ballet was now called, needed new costumes and decor. Diaghilev commissioned these of Matisse, who had never designed specifically for the ballet. Matisse set to work and created a model of the stage so he could make certain the sets and costumes were conceived correctly.

The revised *Nightingale* was first performed in December 1919 in Geneva, then traveled to London and Paris for the 1920 season. Unfortunately, Matisse's decor for the ballet, set in a fairy-tale Chinese court, has also been lost. It featured a turquoise-blue background against which architectural details were juxtaposed. The floor and ceiling were black but festooned with white fabric. The costumes must have been stunning. For the most part they were made up of flowing white robes set off by simple geometric patterns of chevrons and triangles. Matisse also created the design for the stage curtain which featured three large theatrical masks supported by white Chinese griffons with bold, green manes. A scattering of light blue flowers provided the border around the griffons.

In spite of Matisse's striking designs and the entire company's lengthy rehearsals, the production proved a failure, largely because of Massine's experimental choreography. *Song of the Nightingale,* was never presented again after the year of its premier, which may account for the loss of Matisse's sets and costumes.

As a result of work on *Song of the Nightingale* Matisse formed a lasting friendship with the famous Leonide Massine, who choreographed the ballet and who worked closely with Matisse on the sets and costumes. Massine and Diaghilev occasionally visited Matisse in Nice during the Ballets Russes's season in Monte Carlo. Diaghilev undoubtedly hoped to persuade Matisse to design another ballet, but Matisse, perhaps discouraged by the failure of *Song of the Nightingale,* was never to work for the Russian impresario again.

Matisse was, however, at least vaguely associated with a second of Prokofiev's three ballets for the Ballets Russes. Diaghilev attempted to persuade the French artist to design the 1929 premier of Prokofiev's *Prodigal Son*, the last ballet produced by Diaghilev before his death. The collaboration never became a reality; instead the production was designed by another of Matisse's fellow-fauvists, Georges Rouault.

Serge Prokofiev *by Henri Matisse (1921), sketch for Ballets Russes program cover, original lost*

George Gershwin

This new piece, really a rhapsodic ballet, is written very freely and is the most modern music I've yet attempted. The opening part will be developed in typical French style, in the manner of Debussy and the Six, though the themes are all original. My purpose here is to portray the impression of an American visitor in Paris, as he strides about the city, and listens to various street noises and absorbs the French atmosphere.

This is George Gershwin's own description of the programmatic content of *An American in Paris*, which was completed in 1928 and first performed in December of that year (Jablonski, 126). At the beginning of the next year, RCA made a recording of *American*, and Gershwin (1898–1937) began writing *Show Girl*, which would feature Jimmy Durante, Eddie Foy, Ruby Keeler, and the Duke Ellington Orchestra.

In the midst of this musical activity, George Gershwin paused to have his portrait done by the Japanese-American artist Isamu Noguchi (1904–1988). The sculptor had just returned from Paris and set up a studio in Carnegie Hall. While in Paris, Noguchi had been fortunate enough to serve as an apprentice to one of the pioneers in the development of early twentieth-century abstract sculpture, Constantin Brancusi.

Upon his return to the United States, Noguchi turned to portraiture as the best way for a sculptor to earn a living. His friends introduced him to clients, many of whom also became personal friends. Among them were such notables of American culture as Buckminster Fuller, George Gershwin, Martha Graham, Doris Humphrey, Julien Levy, and Nicholas Roerich. Noguchi found in many of his subjects a happy combination of personality and appearance that produced some of the most thoroughly modern examples of early twentieth-century American sculpture.

Portraits were not Noguchi's favorite subject matter, yet he possessed a developed ability to perceive basic structural forms in his sitters' faces. Nothing reflects this better than his 1929 *George Gershwin*. Noguchi took the composer's long head and made a perfect, truncated wedge of it. He smoothed the lines of the neck, cheeks, temples, and skull. When seen from the front, they appear almost straight. The other lines and planes of the face have been simplified to the point of abstraction. Gershwin's upper lip curves sensitively; his eyelids are totally closed so that, with the forward tilt of the head, he appears lost in thought.

It is difficult to identify Noguchi with any particular twentieth-century art movement, primarily because of the extremely personal nature of his artistic vision. Two reasons might be suggested for this: Noguchi's interest in the art of Japan, and his apprenticeship with Brancusi. Both taught him the importance of penetrating to the essence of his subjects; both emphasized the inherent beauty of materials. In the *Gershwin*, it is the dull surface polish given the bronze that adds so much to the portrait's simplicity and abstract treatment of form.

The head was one of fifteen shown by Marie Steiner in a one-person show in 1930 that won Noguchi's first significant critical acclaim in the United States. From there the portrait went on to be exhibited at Harvard University and in the Arts Club of Chicago before coming to reside in Gershwin's personal collection. Period photographs show it on bookshelves in Gershwin's penthouse at 33 Riverside Drive, where it looks perfectly at home in the midst of its art-deco surroundings.

The head was frequently in good company, for Gershwin was also an avid collector and a talented portraitist. Largely on the advice of his cousin, Henry Botkin, a painter who lived in Paris, Gershwin put together a collection that included the work of Chagall, Derain, Kandinsky, Kokoschka, Modigliani, Picasso, Rouault, and Utrillo.

Under the mentorship of his talented cousin, Gershwin learned to paint in a style that might loosely be called expressionist. In the ten years he painted, his work showed increasing insight. Ironically, his favorite subject was portraiture. While he most frequently represented members of his family, he also painted composers' portraits, among them Jerome Kern and Arnold Schoenberg.

George Gershwin *by Isamu Noguchi (1929), bronze, 40 cm, The Israel Museum, Tel-Aviv*

147

Francis Poulenc

"He was in love with life, mischievous, good-hearted, tender and pert, sad and serenely mystical, at once monk and playboy." Stéphane Audel thus described Poulenc in an essay written a few months after the composer's death (Poulenc, 26). The "disconcerting mixture of buffoonery and seriousness" is also mentioned by James Harding in his colorful account of Paris musical life during the twenties.

Cocteau's clever drawing of Poulenc shows the caricaturist's flair for capturing and exaggerating the essential. We see the composer at the piano, looking over his shoulder, presumably at a singer, accompanying what probably is a light song, providing a "vamp" type of rhythmical background.

The popular opinion of Francis Poulenc (1899–1963) tends to stress this lighter side, in part because of the whimsical, ironic quality of some of his songs. This is unfortunate: a considerable portion of his oeuvre is serious and substantial, deeply felt and at times revealing a profoundly religious person. Many of his choral compositions testify to this, as does his opera *Les dialogues des Carmélites*, written in 1953–1955. *La voix humaine* (first performed in 1959) is a heart-rending musical setting of a woman's telephone conversation with her lover whom she fears she is losing. It is a monodrama—a musical tour de force, as we hear only her part of the conversation. The opera is based on a Cocteau play of 1929. Poulenc was glad to have completed the score: "I've had enough of harrowing subjects. When shall I write happy music again?" (Poulenc, 17).

In his early years, Poulenc was a member of that rather informal group of musician-friends who became known as *Les Six* (see p. 150). He described them:

> In a Montparnasse studio, under the title "Lyre et Palette," we became associated with the artists Picasso, Braque, Modigliani, and Juan Gris, who exhibited there.... Our names only had to be linked together as a team several times, for a critic needing a slogan, to baptize [us] *Les Six*, on the model of the famous "Five" Russian composers. (Poulenc, 42)

Poulenc's association with painters is documented in other ways. His choral work *Figure humaine* (text by Paul Éluard, his lifelong friend) is dedicated to Picasso. It is an anguished, poetic work, inspired by feelings of despair during the German occupation of France. Paintings and drawings by Picasso, Braque, Matisse, and Cocteau hung in Poulenc's Paris apartment and his country home. Poulenc's group of songs entitled *Le travail du peintre* (the painter's work, 1956, texts also by Éluard) includes one song devoted to Picasso.

Jean Cocteau (1889–1963) earned honors and distinction chiefly as a poet, playwright, author of film scenarios, and as essayist-philosopher; he also was a graphic artist. In 1911 he began designing posters (for Diaghilev's Ballets Russes), decorative title pages (for books and sheet music), book illustrations, and fashion sketches. He first met Picasso in 1916. Numerous illustrations by Cocteau, including line drawings of the 1920s, remind us of Picasso's similar interest in traditional drawing at this time (see Manuel de Falla, p. 133). Poulenc characterizes Cocteau's relation to *Les Six*: "Cocteau wasn't our theorist, but our friend and brilliant spokesman" (Poulenc, 43). Given the combination of Cocteau's talents and interests, it is not surprising that he should have provided portraits of musicians and other artists of his circle, including drawings of Satie, Georges Auric (of the *Six*), and an often-reproduced portrait of Stravinsky with Picasso. Many of these were included in Cocteau's volume of early drawings entitled *Dessins*, published in 1924 with a dedication to Picasso.

Poulenc was a superb accompanist. Collectors today cherish recordings he made around 1950, many with his friend, the baritone Pierre Bernac. While Poulenc wrote many serious, deeply felt mélodies (the French equivalent of Lieder), our caricature suggests that Cocteau may have had in mind some of his own lighter verses, set by Poulenc in 1919. *Enfant de la troupe* comes to mind, with its circus atmosphere. Like Picasso, Cocteau was fascinated by circuses.

Later Poulenc songs, such as the group *Banalités* of 1940, are similarly wistful. *Voyage à Paris*, slight and very short, serves as an example:

Ah! la charmante chose	Isn't it lovely to leave a
Quitter un pays morose	dreary place
Pour Paris	for Paris,
Paris joli ...	delightful Paris!

A cabaret mood is suggested by the somewhat trivial waltz melody, some touches of jazz in the harmony, and by the repetitive rhythm pattern. Bernac has noted that Poulenc was a friend and fan of Maurice Chevalier, one of the most popular interpreters of cabaret-style songs during the 1940s, in France and in the United States.

Poulenc's association with Cocteau remained a close one. They died within a year of each other, each of a heart attack.

Francis Poulenc, *caricature by Jean Cocteau (1922), first reproduced in Cocteau's* Dessins, *11 × 19 cm, 1924*

Le Groupe des Six

When Louis Durey quit *Les Six* in 1921, he left Jacques-Emile Blanche (1861–1942) only five of their number to paint in this group portrait. From left to right they are: Germaine Tailleferre, Darius Milhaud, Arthur Honegger, Francis Poulenc, Georges Auric. In addition, Marcelle Mayer kneels casually on a chair in the foreground; Jean Cocteau (see p. 148) is pictured in the extreme upper right; finally Jean Wiener stands behind the group, his baton raised.

Two overhead lights and a ring of loge seats arc above Poulenc's and Cocteau's heads. This hint of a concert hall setting suggests a context for the painting: an influential concert of music of *Les Six* sponsored by the conductor Wiener in the early 1920s.

The term *Les Six*, associated with this loose alliance of composers, was coined in 1920 by the critic Henri Collet. The short-lived group lasted no more than a decade (1917–1927). Its members were less responsible for reforming music in France than for extending the French tradition in music. However, Jean Cocteau, the group's self-appointed spokesman for a time, clearly believed *Les Six* stood against the "charm" of Debussy and Ravel.

The beliefs of *Les Six* might best be defined by the composers whose ideas the group rejected, largely under the influence of Cocteau. That author's *Le Coq et l'Arlequin,* published in 1918, attacked the Russians Mussorgski, Rimsky-Korsakov, and Stravinsky, and the Germans Richard Strauss and Wagner—not so much because their music was foreign, but because it was not French.

When members of *Les Six* began to go their own directions, it was, in part, because of their musical tastes. As early as 1921, Durey quit the group, largely because of his appreciation of Ravel, whom the others rejected. Poulenc and Milhaud nurtured an attraction for the work of Schoenberg. Some members of the group also embraced newer ideas, in particular music inspired by the life and sounds of the city. They were equally fascinated by American jazz, and incorporated its melodies and syncopation into their work.

It is difficult to say exactly how these composers met the French portraitist, Jacques-Emile Blanche. It may have been through one of their number, Darius Milhaud, who tells about his first meeting with the artist in his *Notes Without Music:*

It was at [my cousin Xavier Leon's] place that I met Jacques-Emile Blanche. He had a keen taste for music, and often played pianoforte duets with his sisters-in-law.... I liked his studio because "everybody that was somebody" had had his or her portrait done there. You saw Barrès and Debussy next to Bergson or Nijinsky. No sooner had anyone made a name for himself in Paris than Blanche got to know him and paint his portrait. He had an amazing memory and could relate the most wonderfully scathing anecdotes. This intellectual curiosity was aroused by all the latest developments in music, painting, and literature.... (Milhaud, 48)

One of the most popular portraitists of his day, Blanche was also a gifted musician. He played the piano with exceptional dexterity in his youth and was, for a time, devoted to the music of Wagner. Singularly charming, the artist moved with ease in both British and French circles, from whose ranks many of his subjects were drawn. Fellow artists, writers, and musicians also submitted to his discerning eye. Among the more prominent of the cultural elite he painted were Aubrey Beardsley, Paul Claudel, Jean Cocteau, Claude Debussy, Edgar Degas, André Gide, Thomas Hardy, Henry James, James Joyce, Maeterlinck, George Moore, Anna de Noailles, Marcel Proust, Auguste Rodin, Igor Stravinsky, and Virginia Woolf.

Not content only to paint, Blanche also wrote fiction, criticism, art history, and an entertaining set of memoirs, *Portraits of a Lifetime* and *More Portraits of a Lifetime.* Blanche does not recount the circumstances of the sitting for this group portrait in his memoirs, but he does mention the infamous bar *Le Boeuf sur le toit* (the title taken from the Cocteau theater piece, with music by Milhaud), frequented by members of the group:

This was Jean Cocteau's meeting place and also that of the somewhat over-rated musical group the "Six." This group set out to dissipate the mists and languors of Debussy by reinvigorating music as well as poetry in utilizing popular folk-lore, the simple joy discernible in the noises of [the] crowd. (Blanche, 10)

The painter seems to have greater appreciation for ideas that inspired the group than he did for its compositions, but then Blanche's tastes ran more to literature than to music. When in a mood for music, he preferred composers of the nineteenth to those of the twentieth century. In short, Blanche appreciated the very composers whom Cocteau had attacked in *Le Coq et l'Arlequin,* that tract which initially championed *Les Six.*

Le Groupe des Six,
(Hommage à Satie) *by*
Jacques-Emile Blanche
(1922–23), oil on canvas,
188 × 112, Musée des
Beaux-Arts, Rouen

151

Ernst Krenek

*The artist reproduces Nature as he sees it—but he
also sees something which the non-artist cannot
see. The representation of Nature, seen through
the eye of an artist, reveals something of the
mystery of all Being.... The artist's means for
this are stylization and transformation, not
naturalistic imitation.*

ANNA MAHLER, 1962

In her bust of the composer, writer, teacher,
and fellow artist who had once been her husband, Anna Mahler (quoted from Gombrich, 11)
evoked through subtle and bold suggestion the
quiet intensity of this major figure in twentieth-
century music.

Ernst Krenek's long and distinguished career
began in Europe (he was born in Vienna in
1900) where his music was both successful and
controversial. Like Bartók, Schoenberg, Hinde-
mith, and other leading composers, he left his
homeland during the political upheavals of the
1930s and became an American citizen. He continued to compose in virtually all musical genres,
taught at several universities, and wrote books
that convey his ideas on many subjects,
including his impressions of America. He died
on 22 December 1991 in California.

As a man and as a composer, Krenek has
always been keenly interested in the world
around him—in history, politics, geography,
travel. His fascination extends to the means of
travel: trains, planes, cars. He even set to music a
portion of the Santa Fe Railroad timetable
(unaccompanied chorus, 1945). His early and
continuing devotion to history and mythology is
reflected in the subject matter of several operas:
Orpheus and Eurydice (1923, text by the painter
Kokoschka); *The Life of Orestes* (1929); and
Charles V (1933). During the 1940s, Krenek's
interest in medieval and renaissance music also
resulted in a book about the fifteenth-century
composer Johannes Ockeghem. But no single
label such as "neoclassic" would identify
Krenek's own composing. He came to terms
with many musical trends and styles, such as
atonality and serial writing, but his love of
Schubert also inspired him to complete that
composer's unfinished piano sonata in C major
(1922). His opera *Jonny spielt auf* (Jonny strikes
up, 1925), incorporating elements of jazz, was
his greatest success—for the wrong reasons, he

thought (Saathen). Electronic music was still in
its infancy when Krenek began to explore its
possibilities, both in its pure applications and in
combination with traditionally generated
sounds. He wrote a fair number of such works
during the 1950s and thereafter. Krenek also
composed for the equally new medium of
television.

Krenek began to paint and draw during his
childhood and continued, off and on, into his
American years when he painted California
landscapes.

While living in Berlin he had met Anna
Mahler (1904-1988), the younger daughter of
Gustav and Alma Mahler, herself the daughter
of the Austrian painter Emil Jakob Schindler.
Other painters and architects (Kokoschka, Klimt,
Gropius) played important roles in Alma's life;
thus it is not surprising that Anna, too, would
turn to the visual arts. She attended art school in
Berlin, living and working with Krenek. At that
time, painting was her chief interest.

Their marriage (1923) did not last long. Anna
left for Rome where she studied for a short time
with the painter Giorgio di Chirico, and then
moved on to Vienna, Venice, and Paris. In time,
sculpture turned out to be her preferred
medium, in which she was largely self-taught,
though she studied some with the Austrian
sculptor Karl Wotruba. At one time she was
married to Franz Werfel's publisher, Paul
Zsolnay.

Political upheavals leading to the Second
World War contributed to her many changes of
residence. For a while (c. 1950) she taught at the
University of California in Los Angeles. Krenek
recently reminisced: "After Werfel's death, Alma
moved to New York and Anna stayed in Los
Angeles. We were on good terms and visited
once in a while. This is how the bust came about"
(letter to the author). Eventually Anna Mahler
returned to Europe. She died in London in June
1988, shortly before a major exhibit of her works
opened in Salzburg.

Because of her own musicality—she was a fine
pianist—and because of the musical circles in
which she moved, Anna Mahler sculpted busts
of many major musicians of her time, including
Alban Berg (1935); Anatole Fistoulari (1940,
conductor to whom she was married for a short
time); Artur Schnabel (1946, pianist); Otto
Klemperer (1947, conductor); Arnold Schoenberg (1951); Alfred Wallenstein (1951,
conductor); Erich Wolfgang Korngold (1958,
composer); and Rudolf Serkin (1963, pianist).

Ernst Krenek by Anna Mahler (1957), bronze, lifesize, Historisches Museum der Stadt Wien, Vienna

John Cage

No living composer has had greater influence on the arts (both music and the visual arts) than John Cage (1912–), which makes him an especially appropriate figure with whom to close this volume. Quite obviously, Walter De Maria's *Statue of John Cage* does not pretend to present a portrait of the composer in the standard fashion. Rather, De Maria (1935–) takes a more conceptual approach. In making a work fashioned of bars, he may be creating a visual pun on Cage's last name. Clearly, the enigmatic piece was intended as a tribute to Cage; perhaps it even attempts to give visual shape to some of the composer's important ideas concerning structure in a work of art.

A student of Henry Cowell and Arnold Schoenberg (see p. 129), John Cage set forth ideas about structure, chance, freedom, silence, and the *Gesamtkunstwerk*, the total work of art, that have become hallmarks of contemporary art theory. Even more than his daring, notorious compositions, his books, *Silence* and *Empty Words*, have served to make his ideas about the nature and function of art accessible to the curious in all fields of artistic endeavor.

The emphasis on structure visible in De Maria's *Cage* was also important to the young John Cage, who felt that structure was "the proper concern of the mind (as opposed to the heart) (one's ideas of order as opposed to one's spontaneous actions)" (Cage, 18).

Cage found the Orient, in particular ideas derived from Zen Buddhism and the *I Ching*, to offer novel solutions to aesthetic problems. The Zen emphasis on quietude and meditation encouraged him to view silence not as a series of rests in a composition, but rather as the "first inclination of the possibility of saying nothing" (Tomkins, 106). This helped turn the attention of his audiences to an entire range of sounds (or experiences) previously considered outside the realm of art. Indeed, Cage's theories are basic to the continuing redefinition of art that has been so pervasive in contemporary art theory since the 1960s.

As early as 1951, Cage's interest in Oriental philosophy led him to explore chance, or "indeterminacy," as the basis for assembling many of his compositions. Employing chance operations derived from the *I Ching*, Cage would follow the traditional Chinese method of tossing coins or throwing sticks to make decisions involving tempo, pitch, and dynamics in his compositions. Chance became the method by which Cage freed himself from certain decisions necessary in the process of writing music.

Cage had been interested in the visual arts as early as 1942 when various European surrealists came to live in exile in the New York area. For a time, he served as coeditor of the short-lived art journal, *Possibilities*. Cage also presented his ideas to the abstract expressionists at "The Club," and taught at Black Mountain College in the summers of 1948 and 1952. During the latter summer he was largely responsible for staging the first so-called "happening" that brought together artistic personalities as diverse as the poet Charles Olsen, the dancer Merce Cunningham, and the painter Robert Rauschenberg.

De Maria's *Cage* was created in 1962, one year after publication of Cage's most influential book, *Silence*. During 1962 Cage also composed his infamous 4'33", a piano piece in three movements, in which not a single note is played. One of the principal ideas in the piece was simply that any noise inside (or indeed outside) the auditorium could be construed as musical.

A leading figure behind earthworks or earth sculpture, De Maria often combines geometry and measure in ways that might initially seem paradoxical. At its core, however, his art stresses the close relationship between reason and nature.

Cage consists of eight thin poles made of wood. Similar slender cylindrical shapes have been a consistent feature in De Maria's most influential works: *Lightning Field* (1977), *Broken Kilometer* (1979), and *360 I Ching* (1981). Featuring 576 painted white poles forming the sixty-four diagrams of the *I Ching*, *360* clearly illustrates the parallel influence exerted by the *I Ching* on both Cage and De Maria. As do many of De Maria's cylindrical pieces, *360* was intended to emphasize the way the *I Ching* describes the dynamic forces responsible for shaping the world.

To say any more about De Maria's work may defeat one of its chief attributes. In most cases his sculpture, like *Cage*, defies description or aesthetic classification. More than a portrait of the composer, *Cage* represents the time from which it comes, an era of prefabrication, structure, accuracy, and anonymity.

Statue of John Cage *by*
Walter De Maria (1962),
wood, 215.9 cm, private
collection

List of Large Plates

List of Illustrations

Bibliography

Abert, Hermann. *W. A. Mozart.* Leipzig,1956.

Anderson, Emily, ed. *The Letters of Mozart and His Family.* 3 vols. London, 1938.

Angermüller, Rudolph. *Antonio Salieri, sein Leben und seine weltlichen Werke.* 3 vols. Munich, 1971–74.

Anthony, James R. *French Baroque Music from Beaujoyeulx to Rameau.* New York, 1974.

Arnason, H. H. *The Sculptures of Houdon.* New York, 1975.

Arnold, Denis, and Nigel Fortune, eds. *The Monteverdi Companion.* London, 1968.

Arts Council of Great Britain. *Gustave Courbet.* Exhibition catalog, 1980.

Asow, H., and E. H. von Mueller, eds. *The Collected Correspondence and Papers of Christoph Willibald Gluck.* New York, n.d. (German ed. Berlin, 1962).

Audel, Stéphane. See: Poulenc.

Baillio, Joseph. *Elisabeth Louise Vigée Le Brun,1755–1842.* Ft. Worth, 1982.

Barth, H., and D. Mack, eds. *Delius—A Life in Pictures.* London, 1983.

Barth, H., D. Mack, and E. Voss, eds. *Wagner: A Documentary Study.* New York, 1975.

Barzun, Jacques. *Berlioz and the Romantic Century.* 2 vols. New York, 1950.

Bassi, Elena. *Canova.* Bergamo, 1943.

Baumann, E. *La vie terrible d'Henry de Groux.* Paris, 1936.

Beaumont, Anthony. *Busoni, the Composer.* London, 1985.

Beecham, Sir Thomas. *Frederick Delius.* New York, 1960.

Benesch, Otto. "Schütz and Rembrandt." *Collected Writings.* Vol. 1. London, 1970, 228–234.

Benton, Thomas H. *An Artist in America.* New York, 1937.

Bernac, Pierre. *Francis Poulenc: The Man and His Songs.* London, 1978.

Bernard, Jonathan W. *The Music of Edgard Varèse.* New Haven, 1987.

Beyle, Henri. See: Stendhal.

Biba, Otto. "Einige neue und wichtige Schubertiana . . ." *Oesterreichische Musikzeitschrift* 33 (1978): 604–610.

_____. "Neues aus dem Archiv." *Oesterreichische Musikzeitschrift* 32 (1977): 90–92.

Bischoff, Friedrich. " 'Dire que maintenant . . .' Eine Daumier-Karikatur von Berlioz, Wagner und Rossini." *Die Musikforschung* 38 (1985): 22–26.

Blanche, Jacques-Emile. *More Portraits of a Lifetime, 1918–1938.* Tr. W. Clement. London, 1939.

Blaukopf, Herta. *Gustav Mahler Briefe.* Vienna, 1982.

Blaukopf, Kurt, ed. *Mahler, a Documentary Study.* New York, 1976.

Blunt, Wilfred. *On Wings of Song: A Biography of Felix Mendelssohn.* London, 1974.

Bolliger, Hans, and Bernhard Geiser. *Pablo Picasso: 55 Years of His Graphic Work.* Stuttgart, 1965.

Bondeville, Emmanuel. "Eugène Delacroix, musicien, critique musical, professeur de composition." *Institut de France. Académie des Beaux-Arts. Année 1963–1964.* Paris, 1964, 19–26.

Boyd, Malcolm. *Domenico Scarlatti: Master of Music.* New York, 1987.

Brattskoven, Otto. " 'Mopp' (Max Oppenheimer)." *The Studio* 92 (July–December 1926): 267–271.

Braunbehrens, Volkmar. *Salieri: Ein Musiker im Schatten Mozarts.* Munich, 1989.

Brody, Elaine. "Paris, 1840." *American Scholar* 53 (Winter 1983): 83–90.

_____. *Paris, the Musical Kaleidoscope 1870–1925.* New York, 1987.

Bruyn, J., B. Haak, S. H. Levie, P. J. J. Van Thiel, and E. Van de Wetering. *A Corpus of Rembrandt Paintings.* Vol. 1. Amsterdam, 1986.

Burney, Charles. *A General History of Music.* Ed. Frank Mercer. 2 vols. New York, 1957 (1st publ. 1776–1789).

Cabanne, Pierre. *Le siècle de Picasso.* 2 vols. Paris, 1975.

Cage, John. *Silence.* Cambridge, MA, 1961.

Canova, Antonio. *L'opera completa del Canova.* Milan, 1976.

_____. *The works of Antonio Canova with descriptions from the Italian of the Countess Albrizzi.* 2 vols. Boston, 1876.

Carley, Lionel. *Delius: A Life in Letters, 1909–1934.* Cambridge, England, 1988.

———. *Delius: The Paris Years.* London, 1975.

Carr, C. K., and M. C. S. Christman. *Gaston Lachaise: Portrait Sculpture.* Washington, D.C., 1985.

Charteris, Evan. *John Sargent.* New York, 1927. Reprint, 1972.

Chiesa, Maria Tibaldi. *Cimarosa e il suo tempo.* Milan, 1939.

Chissell, Joan. *Clara Schumann: A Dedicated Spirit.* London, 1983.

———. *Schumann.* New York, 1967.

Clark, Anthony, *Pompeo Batoni.* New York, 1985.

Clark, T. J. *Image of the People: Gustave Courbet and the 1848 Revolution.* Princeton, 1973.

Cocteau, Jean. *Dessins.* Paris, 1924.

———. "Introductory Speech." In *Le groupe des Six.* Angel Records (Album 3515-B). New York, 1953.

Comini, Alessandra. *The Changing Image of Beethoven: A Study in Myth-Making.* Dallas, 1986.

———. "The Visual Brahms: Idols and Images." *Arts Magazine* 54 (October 1979): 123–129.

———. "Through a Viennese Looking-Glass Darkly: Images of Arnold Schönberg and His Circle." *Arts Magazine* 58 (May 1984): 107–119.

Conati, Marcell, ed. *Encounters with Verdi.* Tr. Richard Stores. Ithaca, NY, 1984.

Condon, Patricia. *In Pursuit of Perfection: The Art of J. A. D. Ingres.* Louisville, KY, 1983.

Cooper, Martin. *Gluck.* New York, 1935. Reprint, 1978.

———. *Russian Opera.* London, 1951.

Coopersmith, J. M. "A List of Portraits, Sculpture, etc. of G. F. Handel." *Music and Letters* 13 (1932): 156 ff.

Cortot, Alfred. *In Search of Chopin.* New York, 1952.

Courcy, G. I. C. *Paganini: The Genoese.* Norman, OK, 1957.

Courthion, Pierre. "Courbet as a Portrait Painter." *Courbet in Perspective.* Ed. Petra T. Chu. Englewood Cliffs, 1977.

Cranston, Maurice. *Jean-Jacques: The Early Life and Work of Jean-Jacques Rousseau, 1712–1754.* London, 1982.

Dean, Winton. *The New Grove Handel.* London, 1982.

Deane, Basil. *Cherubini.* Oxford, 1965.

Debussy, Claude. *Debussy Letters.* Eds. François Lesure and Roger Nichols, tr. Roger Nichols. Cambridge, MA, 1987.

Delacroix, Eugène. *The Journal of Eugène Delacroix.* Ed. Hubert Wellington. Ithaca, NY, 1951; rev. ed., 1980.

Delage, Roger. *Iconographie musicale: Chabrier.* N.p., 1982.

Demarquez, Suzanne. *Manuel de Falla.* Philadelphia, 1968.

Deutsch, Otto Erich. "Beethovens Leben in Bildern." *Österreichische Musikzeitschrift* 16, 3 March 1961.

———. *Handel: A Documentary Biography.* New York, 1974 (1st ed. 1955).

———. *Mozart: Die Dokumente seines Lebens.* Kassel, 1961.

———. *Mozart und seine Welt in zeitgenössischen Bildern.* Kassel, 1961.

———. *The Schubert Reader.* Tr. Eric Blom. New York, 1947.

Diderot, Denis. *Oeuvres complètes de Diderot.* Paris, 1875–77. Reprint, 1960.

Dies, A. C. "Biographische Nachrichten von Joseph Haydn." Vienna, 1810. English tr. in V. Gotvals, ed. *Joseph Haydn: Eighteenth-Century Gentleman and Genius.* Madison, 1963.

Dietschy, Marcel. *La Passion de Claude Debussy.* Neuchatel, 1962.

Dittersdorf, Karl von. *The Autobiography of Karl von Dittersdorf.* Tr. A. D. Coleridge. London, 1896. Reprint, New York, 1970.

Einstein, Alfred. *Gluck.* London, 1936. Reprint, 1954.

Endler, Franz. *Vienna: A Guide to its Music and Musicians.* Portland, OR, 1989.

Ewen, David. *George Gershwin: His Journey to Greatness.* Westport, CT, 1970.

Fleury, E. and G. Brière. *Catalogue, Collection Maurice-Quentin Delatour à Saint-Quentin.* Saint Quentin, 1954.

Flotzinger, Rudolf, and Gernot Gruber. "Die Avantgarde." *Musikgeschichte Österreichs* (1979): 433 ff.

Freitag, Eberhard. *Schönberg als Maler.* Diss. Vienna, 1973.

Frimml, Theodor. *Beethovens äussere Erscheinung* (Beethoven Studien I). Munich, 1905.

Gal, Hans. *Letters of the Great Composers.* London, 1965. Reprint, 1978.

Garden, Edward. *Tchaikovsky.* London, 1973.

Gartenberg, Egon. *Mahler: The Man and His Music.* New York, 1978.

Gärtner, Heinz. *Johann Christian Bach.* Munich, 1989. English tr. Portland, OR, 1992.

Geck, Martin. *Die Bildnisse Richard Wagners.* Munich, 1970.

Gerber, Rudolf. *Christoph Willibald Gluck.* Potsdam, 1950.

Girdlestone, Cuthbert. *Jean-Phillipe Rameau.* London, 1957.

———. "Rameau, Jean-Philippe." *The New Grove Dictionary of Music and Musicians.* London, 1980.

Gombrich, Ernst H., ed. *Anna Mahler: Her Work.* Stuttgart, 1975.

Gounod, Charles. *Autobiographical Reminiscences with Family Letters and Notes on Music.* Tr. W. H. Hutchinson. London, 1896.

Gowers, Patrick. "Erik Satie." *The New Grove Dictionary of Music and Musicians.* London, 1980.

Gray, Camilla. *The Great Experiment: Russian Art 1863–1923.* New York, 1962.

Griesinger, G. A. "Biographische Notizen über Joseph Haydn." Leipzig, 1809. English tr. in V. Gotvals, ed. *Joseph Haydn: Eighteenth-Century Gentleman and Genius.* Madison, 1963.

Grote. *Memoir of the Life of Ary Scheffer.* London, 1860.

Grunfeld, Frederic. *Rodin: A Biography.* New York, 1987.

Gutman, Robert W. *Richard Wagner: The Man, His Mind, and His Music.* New York, 1968.

Gutmann, Danièle. "Rodin et la musique." *Revue internationale de musique française* 7 (1982): 103–113.

Hahl-Koch, Jelena, ed. *Arnold Schoenberg-Wassili Kandinsky: Briefe, Bilder und Dokumente einer aussergewöhnlichen Begegnung.* Salzburg, 1981. English tr. John C. Crawford. London, 1984.

Harding, James. *Erik Satie.* London, 1975.

———. *Gounod.* New York, 1973.

———. *The Ox on the Roof.* New York, 1986.

Hawkins, John. *A General History of the Science and Practice of Music.* London, 1776.

Hayes, John. *Gainsborough.* New York, 1975.

Hevesi, Ludwig, ed. *Victor Tilgners ausgewählte Werke.* Vienna, 1897.

Hilmar, Ernst, ed. *Arnold Schönberg Gedenkausstellung.* Vienna, 1974.

Horgan, Paul. *Encounters with Stravinsky: A Personal Record.* New York, 1972.

Hubbard, Elbert. *Little Journeys to the Homes of Eminent Painters.* New York, n.d. (1899).

Huyghe, René. *Delacroix.* New York, 1963.

Isherwood, Robert. *Music in the Service of the King.* Ithaca, NY, 1973.

Jablonski, Edward, and Lawrence Stewart. *The Gershwin Years.* New York, 1973.

Jacob, Heinrich. *Felix Mendelssohn and His Times.* Tr. R. and C. Winston. Englewood Cliffs, 1963.

Jenkins, David and Mark Visocchi. *Mendelssohn in Scotland.* London, 1978.

Johnson, Harold E. *Jean Sibelius.* New York, 1959.

Johnson, Lee. *The Paintings of Eugène Delacroix.* 4 vols. Oxford, 1981.

Junod, Philippe. *La musique vue par les peintres.* Lausanne, 1988.

Kallir, Jane. *Arnold Schoenberg's Vienna.* Exhibition catalog. New York, 1984.

Kapp, Julius. *Paganini.* Berlin, 1913.

Kimball, Robert, and Alfred Simon. *The Gershwins.* New York, 1973.

Kinsky, Georg. *A History of Music in Pictures.* London, 1937.

Kirkpatrick, Ralph. *Domenico Scarlatti.* Princeton, 1953.

Kobald, Karl. *Schubert und Schwind: ein Wiener Biedermeierbuch.* Zurich, 1921.

Koechlin, Charles. *Gabriel Fauré.* Tr. Leslie Orrey. London, 1946.

Kokoschka, Oskar. *Mein Leben.* Munich, 1971. English tr. London, 1974.

Kolneder, Walter. *Antonio Vivaldi.* Wiesbaden, 1965. English tr. Berkeley, 1970.

Kostelanetz, Richard, ed. *John Cage.* New York, 1970.

Krause, Ernst. *Richard Strauss: The Man and His Work.* London, 1964.

Krenek, Ernst. *Music Here and Now.* New York, 1939 (reissued 1967).

———. *Zur Sprache gebracht. Essays über Musik.* Munich, 1958.

Ladenburger, Michael. "Joseph Haydn in zeitgenössischen Abbildungen." *Joseph Haydn in seiner Zeit.* Exhibition catalog. Eisenstadt, 1982, 301–310.

Lalo, Pierre. *De Rameau à Ravel.* Paris, 1947.

Lance, Evelyn. "Molière the Musician." *Music Review* 35 (1974): 120 ff.

Landon, H. C. Robbins. *Beethoven.* New York, 1970.

———. *Handel and His World.* Boston, 1984.

Lang, Paul Henry. *George Frideric Handel.* New York, 1966.

——— and Otto Bettmann. *A Pictorial History of Music.* New York, 1960.

Lapauze, Henry. *Ingres.* Paris, 1911.

László, Z., and B. Mátéka. *Franz Liszt: sein Leben in zeitgenössischen Bildern.* Kassel, 1969.

Lavagnino, Emilio. "Canova." *Encyclopedia of World Art.* New York, 1960.

Lesure, François, ed. *Claude Debussy, Lettres 1884–1918.* Paris, 1980.

Léger, Charles. *Courbet.* Paris, 1929

Licht, Fred, and David Finn. *Canova.* New York, 1983.

Libdin, Laurence. "A Rediscovered Portrait of Rameau." *Early Music* II (1983): 510–513.

Lindsay, Jack. *Gustave Courbet: His Life and Art.* New York, 1973.

———. *Thomas Gainsborough.* New York, 1980.

Lockspeiser, Edward. *Debussy: His Life and Mind.* New York, 1962–65.

Lyaskouskaya, O. *Ilya Repin: His Life and His Work.* Moscow, 1982.

MacDonald, Malcolm. *Brahms.* New York, 1990.

———. *Schoenberg.* London, 1976.

Mack, Gerstle. *Gustave Courbet.* Westport, CT, 1951.

Mahler, Anna. *Die Bildhauerin Anna Mahler.* Salzburg, 1989.

Mainwaring, John. *Memoirs of the Life of the Late George Frideric Handel.* London, 1760. Reprint, New York, 1980.

Marek, George. *Beethoven: Biography of a Genius.* New York, 1969.

———. *Richard Strauss: The Life of a Non-Hero.*

Whitley, William T. *Thomas Gainsborough.* London, 1915.

Wildenstein, Georges. *Ingres.* New York, 1956.

Williamson, George C., ed. *Bryan's Dictionary of Painters and Engravers.* New York, 1972.

Wingler, Hans Maria. *Oskar Kokoschka, das Werk des Malers.* Salzburg, 1956.

Wolf, G. J. "Max Oppenheimer." *Kunst für Alle* 41 (1925–26): 208–215.

Wood, Vivian. *Poulenc's Songs.* Jackson, MS, 1979.

Wynne, Michael. "Hugh Howard: Irish Portrait Painter." *Apollo* 90 (1969): 314–317.

Yastrebtsev, V. V. *Reminiscences of Rimsky-Korsakov.* Ed. and tr. F. Jonas. New York, 1985.

Zimmerman, Franklin. *Henry Purcell, 1659–1695: His Life and Times.* New York, 1967.

Index